W9-CEW-414

The Mate Map

The Right Tool for
Choosing the Right Mate

STEVEN SACKS

Mate Map Enterprises
A division of Banner Publishing
New York

Published by: Mate Map Enterprises, a division of Banner Publishing, 145 E. 16th Street, New York, NY 10003 U.S.A.
Mate Map is a trademark of Mate Map Enterprises.

Interior Design and Typesetting by Desktop Miracles, Inc., Stowe, VT

This book describes the ideas and opinions of its author and is designed to provide commonsense information in the area of relationships. Neither the author nor the publisher is engaged in rendering therapeutic or other professional services in this book. Any reader who requires therapeutic or other professional assistance should consult a therapist or other appropriate professional.

The examples and anecdotes presented in this book are based on the experiences of real people, but names, identifying information and nonessential facts have been changed throughout to protect their privacy. Any similarity to actual individuals is, accordingly, entirely coincidental.

Library of Congress Control Number: 2002090541
Printed in the United States of America
Printed on acid-free paper

First Banner Publishing Edition, 2002

10 9 8 7 6 5 4 3 2 1

Discounts on bulk quantities of books are available to corporations, associations, universities, and other organizations. For details and discount information, contact the sales department of Mate Map Enterprises at 212–592–9057 or info@matemap.com

The Mate Map is available at your local bookstore, and can also be ordered directly through Mate Map Enterprises by calling toll-free at 877–MATE–MAP or visiting our website at www.MATEMAP.com

*I dedicate this book in memoriam to my grandparents,
Sylvia and David Sacks, and Peggy and Joe Frankel,
who thrived in loving relationships and established
a path for the rest of our family to follow.*

Dear Reader,

Welcome to *The Mate Map*, a remarkable new approach to relationships that will help you choose a mate who is right for you.

Too often, people end up in relationships that are bad for them because they did not enter into the relationship knowing *specifically* what they were looking for in a significant other. As a result, these people either suffer through the pain of a breakup or, perhaps worse, remain in a relationship where they are unhappy and unfulfilled.

Don't let this happen to you! No matter what your age or what stage you are in finding a mate, you owe it to yourself to use the Mate Map so you can choose a person with whom you can have a loving and lasting relationship.

If you're currently single and looking for a mate, the Mate Map will help you clarify what you're looking for. Then, when you meet someone special, you'll be prepared to decide whether to give the green light to a potential relationship or to move on in your search for someone who's right for you.

If you're currently in a relationship, the Mate Map will help you understand why you're with this person and help you decide if you want to take the relationship to the next level. It will also reveal any problems with the relationship and show you how to create an action plan for improving them.

Whether you choose to just read *The Mate Map* and use its principles to help you select the right mate or decide to dig in and develop a customized Mate Map, you'll find the information in this book will help you for years to come.

Steven Sacks

Contents

PART THREE
_____

The Mate Map: Phases II, III, IV and V

The Mate Map

Foreword

We all share the same simple desire—to have another person to love. Although what we want is uncomplicated, the path to getting there is often complex. The reason is that there are many barriers along the way that prevent us from finding someone with whom we are truly compatible. Unfortunately, these barriers are seldom obvious to us. Once you realize how many barriers there are, and how difficult they are to overcome, it's no wonder that so many people become entrenched in bad relationships, and that more than half of all marriages end before reaching "happily ever after."

One such barrier for most of us is a near-total lack of structure in the mate-selection process. As I tell the patients in my practice, if you want a fulfilling relationship, you need to create a vision of the relationship you desire. It doesn't just happen. It is especially helpful to make a written record of your vision as a reference to keep you focused on getting the relationship you want.

Another barrier to finding an ideal relationship is that we often make wrong assumptions. For example, when meeting a possible new love interest, we often identify one or two traits we like (or dislike) and then assume we know all about the person in other, totally unrelated areas. We stereotype and try to make predictions because we don't want to waste our time, and understandably so. However, assuming that someone who is kind-hearted will also be affectionate, for example, doesn't help us because it isn't necessarily accurate and can set us up for disappointment. It's far better to examine someone's kind-heartedness and capacity for affection separately, so that we know for sure how compatible we are in both areas.

A third barrier to choosing a good partner is that it's very difficult to be objective. When we begin dating someone, our outlook becomes skewed because the powerful forces of lust affect us. We're driven by our hearts and our hormones, not our heads. As a result, we are unable to make smart relation-ship decisions. We must find a way to overcome the euphoria stage, because objectivity is key to successful mate selection. As I mention in my book *Make Up, Don't Break Up*, studies have shown that, when we are in the euphoria stage, our parents can pick better partners for us than we can because they're armed with objectivity, whereas we don't have the ability to think rationally.

Reaching a high level of overall compatibility with someone is not necessarily achieved by simply having many similarities and few differences, although many believe this to be true. This fallacy is another barrier to finding the right person.

Differences can be beneficial in that they can be comple-mentary. For example, if one person is high-strung, it's often better to pick a person who is more even-keeled, so they can balance out each other. Two people who are too alike can clash because there is not enough give and take in the rela-tionship. This would be the case if, for example, you and your mate both have dominating personalities. Similarly, two peo-ple who are too different can clash because their differences get in the way of their compatibility. For example, if one per-son is the life of the party and the other person is a wallflower, they may get along on some levels, but this difference may cause enough of a problem that it makes them incompatible.

However, deciding which differences are positive indicators of compatibility and which ones are negative is easier said than done. During my office and phone therapy sessions, my patients consistently express their frustration over this dilemma by complaining; "I feel like giving up, it's too hard."

With *The Mate Map*, Steven Sacks helps singles who want a relationship as well as those already in a relationship "figure it all out" by breaking down the barriers to finding the right mate. *The Mate Map* provides a structure that will help you recognize your ideal mate; it will enable you to make accurate assessments about the character and personality traits of a potential mate; and it will lead you to far greater objectivity in contemplating any relationship, new or ongoing. **This groundbreaking book will actually change the way you think about relationships!**

Many of my patients who are long-term single, newly single, or in a stable relationship, have longed for a "map" to lead them to the right person or reassure them that they are with the right person. *The Mate Map* can help you overcome the fears and uncertainties that always accompany the search for the right mate. These fears and uncertainties can cause you to be tentative or avoid relationships altogether, especially if you are separated, divorced or have had a long-term relationship end. But *The Mate Map* will calm your fears. The information you get from this book and the personal Mate Map you create will give you confidence that you will finally find someone who is right for you. You'll know you are addressing everything about your relationship that is within your power to evaluate or change. After using *The Mate Map* you will never again second-guess your relationship decisions.

I believe that Steven Sacks is a trailblazer. In his book for both men and women, you will follow the easy steps to help you select the right mate and build a lasting relationship. Along the way you will find many examples that help bring the details of the mate selection process to life. Now, you too can be a trailblazer by using *The Mate Map* to create your path to the right mate.

The Mate Map **is the most effective tool for determining compatibility and measuring what's important in a relationship that I've ever seen.** Anyone who desires a long-term relationship and struggles with the complexities of finding the right mate owes it to herself or himself to read this book!

No relationship is without flaws, and some relationships fail no matter what we do. But in order to have the best chance of long-term relationship success, the right relationship must start with the right person. By using *The Mate Map*, you will be putting the relationship odds in your favor.

Bonnie Eaker Weil, Ph.D.
Best-selling author of *Make Up, Don't Break Up: Finding and Keeping Love for Singles and Couples* and *Adultery—The Forgivable Sin*
www.makeupdontbreakup.com

Introduction

The Story of the Mate Map

Over the years, I've struggled to find a mate with whom I was confident I could have a fulfilling and lasting relationship. At times I've been single and actively looking for a relationship, while at other times I've been in serious relationships. In both cases, it seemed as though every month I had a new relationship concern.

When I was single and looking, my concerns included:

- "I'm not sure what I want in a mate."
- "Will I ever find someone I'll like enough to want to spend the rest of my life with?"
- "If I find someone, how will I know if she is good for me?"

When I was in a relationship, my concerns included:

- "How fulfilled am I in this relationship?"
- "Something is wrong with this relationship but I can't figure out what it is."
- "At what point should I give up on trying to make this relationship work and accept that it was not meant to be?"
- "How do I know if she's 'the one'?"

Like many other men in their 20s and 30s, I spent my leisure time on such activities as playing golf, going to bars and enjoying "couch time" in front of the TV every Sunday during football season. However, I also spent an abundant amount of time thinking about relationships. Finding someone with whom I wanted to spend the rest of my life was very important to me, so I took it very seriously. By logging an incredible number of hours thinking about and analyzing relationships, I gradually came to understand myself better and learned to make better relationship decisions. However, I still didn't have confidence in my ability to choose the right mate. So I decided to start an open dialog with friends and colleagues about this subject.

When I discussed my mate-selection struggles with others, I discovered there were a lot of people asking themselves the same questions, and that they too were unable to find answers. During continued discussions I realized all of us had the belief that, when we were with someone who was right for us, we would know it because it would just "feel right."

But after thinking more about it, I realized choosing a mate because she "feels right" was not a strong enough basis for choosing one particular person with whom to spend the rest of my life. Yes, this intuition should be part of the mate-selection process, but not to the extent that most people rely on it. I knew that I needed to be more thorough in my reasoning before making such a monumental decision. The question I then asked myself was, "but what specifically can I do to be more thorough?"

Figuring that someone surely must have created a simple, yet thorough, process for choosing a mate, I headed to my local bookstore to find it. Although the shelves were full of relationship books, there was nothing like what I was looking for. I continued my quest by calling a wide variety of bookstores and searching on the internet, and still I found nothing remotely close to what I needed. Next I headed to the library. There I searched through many psychological journals, but only saw studies that reported findings and opinions about other people's relationships—a far cry from what I wanted, which was a system that would help me find someone who was specifically right for me. Finally I realized that, if I wanted a system for choosing the right person for me, I was going to have to create it myself. And that's what I set out to do—find a better way of choosing a mate.

The Analytical Difference

In addition to drawing on my past relationship experiences, my abundant thinking around my relationship concerns, and my relationship discussions with others, I also took advantage of my analytical abilities while creating a new approach to mate selection. Throughout my life I've always looked at problems by breaking them down into smaller components, examining the causes and effects of these components, and proposing changes that would lead to a better outcome. This unique way of looking at the world was apparent at an early age. As my parents tell the story: "When Steven was six years old, we asked him, 'Should we go to the amusement park or the zoo today?' We expected a simple answer of 'amusement park' or 'zoo,' but Steven replied with a thoughtful analysis. 'Well, it depends on what we want to do,' he told us. 'If we want to be active, then we should go to the amusement park. But if we just want to watch, then the zoo would be better.'" I've been looking at the world this way ever since.

I enhanced my analytical abilities through my academic and professional experiences. I have undergraduate and graduate degrees in business, which have provided me with outstanding skills in the areas of strategy, process improvement, and decision making. I've also worked in the business world for ten years for both Fortune 100 companies and small companies, where I honed these skills. It's true that relationships and business are vastly different from one another. However, I knew that certain analytical approaches I had developed in the business world could also be used to improve the world of relationships.

Through all of these experiences, I learned that one of the primary reasons people make bad decisions—whether it's regarding business, relationships, or any other area of life—is that their approach to decision making lacks a structure. By "structure," I mean an organized set of guidelines and processes that is used to reach a specific goal.

Therefore, upon setting out to find a better way of choosing a mate, the first guideline I established was that a structure is needed for the mate-selection process. This structure would help me to prioritize my views regarding a potential or current mate and ultimately prepare me to make a decision about beginning or deepening a relationship.

The second guideline I established was that the new approach to mate selection needs to be individualized. Every two people have a unique relationship, so my approach had to allow me to customize my mate-selection process. There are many small—yet critical—details that vary from one relationship to another, and I realized that, the more closely I examined these details, the more accurate I could be when it came time to select a mate.

After establishing these guidelines, I proceeded to build this new approach to mate selection, which over the years has evolved to become the Mate Map.

Putting the Mate Map to Work

A couple of years ago I went on several dates with a woman—let's call her Jennifer—whom I had met through a mutual friend. There were a lot of things about her I liked, but there were also things I didn't like. What I couldn't figure out was whether the negative aspects were areas I should just chalk up to, "Well, nobody is perfect and no relationship is perfect," and deal with them, or whether these areas were real problems that made us incompatible.

In theory, it seemed that I should know the difference between the two. But, in reality, relationships are one big gray area. To help me turn this gray area into areas that were more black and white, I used the Mate Map for the first time in a real situation. What I discovered was that, although Jennifer and I were a good fit in several areas (she was mature, independent, and physically attractive), we were incompatible in other areas (she held grudges, was too impulsive, and was pessimistic).

In thinking through both the compatible and incompatible areas, I realized that each of the incompatible areas was more important to me than those where we were compatible. When I concluded the fit wasn't there, these incompatible areas became dealbreakers and I stopped dating her. Ending things was not easy, because I had gotten to know Jennifer well and cared about her. But since I had examined the relationship so thoroughly using the Mate Map, I knew that I was doing the best thing long-term for both of us. It was the first time I didn't second-guess a relationship decision I had made. If only I'd had the Mate Map during my earlier relationships!

I continued to use the Mate Map as I dated various women and, finally, one day, when I "mapped" a cute, smart, fun and lovable brunette, I found myself with a Mate Map filled with positive indicators. A few months later we decided to date exclusively. We are still in love and still compatible in all the areas that are most important to me. I consider myself a very fortunate (not to mention happy and fulfilled) man.

After my own success with the Mate Map, I decided to share it with several friends, colleagues, and acquaintances. As I suspected, they also found it extremely helpful in understanding what they wanted out of a relationship and determining what type of person they wanted to be with. My friend Melissa told me, "I just started using the Mate Map a few days ago and already I see my relationship with Greg [her boyfriend] more clearly." An acquaintance, Russell, declared, "I finally stopped dating this girl because the Mate Map showed me I was going out with her for all of the wrong reasons."

The Mate Map Study

During January and February 2002, I conducted the Mate Map Study under the supervision of New York psychologist and statistician Dr. James A. Twaite. The results of the study showed that the Mate Map was effective in achieving its three objectives: (1) The Mate Map increased participants' ability to know what is important to them in a mate; (2) it also increased their confidence in being able to choose a mate that is right for them; and (3) it helped them to identify and improve problem areas in relationships.

The study showed that 87% of the study participants found the Mate Map increased their confidence in understanding what the most important aspects of a relationship are to them; 75% stated that the Mate Map increased their confidence in being able to choose the right mate; and 77% stated that the Mate Map increased their confidence in being able to improve a relationship by identifying and fixing any problem areas. Furthermore, 4 out of 5 participants recommend the Mate Map to their friends. Additional information about the study, including quantitative and qualitative data, can be found in Appendix A.

The study confirmed that what I had created was a very effective way to help people who struggle with dating and relationships. What about you? Unless you are already in a perfect long-term relationship, the Mate Map can help you too—you can find the right mate or determine if you've already found the right person in your current significant other. Read on and learn how to use this remarkable new tool to help you achieve the most important and satisfying goal in your life.

ONE

The Relationship Essentials

1

Mate Selection Gone Bad— Until Now

Boy meets girl. Boy and girl fall in love. Boy and girl live happily ever after.

If this scenario were true of all intimate relationships, life would be better. More of us would be in happy and fulfilling relationships that last a lifetime. But in reality, though great relationships do exist, less-than-great ones are more often the case. Even so, most of us strive to have great relationships. After all, we are put on this planet to enjoy the time we spend on it, and a major part of enjoying life is having someone special to share it with.

Intimate relationships, or simply "relationships," are considered so desirable that every year millions of people decide to have their relationship legally sanctioned by getting married. According to the latest data from the U.S. Census Bureau, every year 4 million people get married in the United States. This number has remained steady over the fifteen-year period of 1986–2000. Unfortunately, over this same fifteen-year period, the rate of divorce has remained steady as well, with 2.2 million people getting divorced year in and year out. This means that more than half of all marriages, 55%, end in divorce.

What about the 45% who stay married? Are they happy? Not as much as one might think. In a 1998 study conducted by the National Opinion Research Center of the University of Chicago, fewer than two thirds of married couples (63.5%) said they were "very happy." Perhaps not surprisingly, the level of "very happy" marriages has consistently been less than stellar over a similar fifteen-year period (1984–1998), ranging from a high of 66% to a low of 60%.

If we use marriage and divorce statistics as benchmarks of relationship desirability and relationship success, we come to two realizations. First, people consistently believe in the benefits of a long-term relationship. Second, there is something wrong with the way many of us approach a relationship, because more than half of our relationships are not working out in the long term. In other words, the lure of relationships remains high, but the success rate remains low.

Compatibility Is the Key

I believe that the primary reason relationships fail is that at least one person in the relationship has chosen someone with whom they are not compatible. Sure, most couples have at least a few areas of *minor* incompatibility, but unless there is a high level of *overall* compatibility, the relationship is not likely to leave you with feelings of happiness and fulfillment. According to a Gallup poll in the late 1980s, "incompatibility" was the number one reason that couples get divorced. While some couples may become incompatible over time, many couples never reach a high level of compatibility in the first place. It's amazing that so many couples with poor compatibility marry, but the truth is that most people literally don't know how to determine if they are compatible with someone else. Luckily, the Mate Map is now available to show you how to determine your overall level of compatibility with your potential or current mate.

But why is it so difficult for us to choose compatible mates in the first place? After all, we all have definite likes and dislikes, and usually have a pretty good idea how those preferences match up with those of other people. I believe the problem in transferring those known preferences to choosing a mate is that there is no formal structure to the way we think about relationships. It is only with a formal structure that we are forced to examine many critical details about our wants and desires, which otherwise get ignored or are examined only marginally. And it is these details that, in many instances, determine true compatibility.

The Nebulous Zone

When we think about dating and relationships, we usually think about them in a very nebulous way. Say I am interested in Allison. My thoughts about her may center on her bright smile and her great sense of humor. I'm also vaguely aware that she is worldly and values education. But these random bits of information do not really help me determine if I want her to be my mate.

In order to think about this potential relationship in a more productive way, I need a structure in which to group my thoughts about Allison. Until now, there has not been a systematic structure for thinking about relationships. Over the years, each of us has had to learn through experience how to deal with dating and having relationships. Whenever we have thought about dating and relationships, we've collected information in random bits and pieces. I call this random collection of information about dating and relationships the **Nebulous Zone**.

What we need to do is take the information in the Nebulous Zone and organize it so we can use it efficiently. The Mate Map provides such an organizing structure, allowing us to think through the many aspects of relationships in ways that will help us identify the right person for us.

The **Mate Map Principles** are general guidelines to keep us focused on the *overall aspects* of relationships that matter most. These Principles are then applied to a system called the **Mate Map**, which helps us focus on the important *details* of what we truly want in a mate, while enabling us to determine how compatible we are with a particular person. I will explain the Mate Map Principles in Chapters 2 through 5, and the actual Mate Map in Chapters 6 through 14.

2

The Mate Map Principles

Using the Mate Map Principles, your path to choosing the right person for a lasting relationship is as easy as **1**, **2**, **3**. The number **1** goal is to fulfill your relationship needs. The **2** ways to examine a relationship are to use intuition and rational thinking, and find a balance between the two. The **3** critical areas in which to assess a mate are Personality Fit, Magnetism and Love.

In the remainder of this chapter we will examine **1** Fulfillment of Needs, **2** Intuition and Rational Thinking, and **3** Personality Fit, Magnetism and Love. In the three chapters that immediately follow this one, we'll look at Personality Fit, Magnetism and Love individually and in detail.

MATE MAP PRINCIPLE I
Fulfill your needs.

When relationships end, it is usually the case that one or both members of the couple thought they were with the right person at some point, but ended up realizing that their mate did not fulfill their relationship needs. This lack of fulfillment manifests itself in a variety of ways (such as an increase in the frequency and intensity of arguments, anxiety or infidelity), and eventually leads to the end of the relationship.

In order to avoid such an outcome, we must make sure we choose a mate who fulfills our needs. In simple terms, if a mate fulfills our needs, we should pursue a relationship with him or her, and if a mate does not fulfill our needs, we should end that relationship and move on to find someone else who does. To know if someone meets our needs, **the first step is to identify exactly what our needs are.** While most of us know generally what we want in a mate, we don't really know enough about what we are looking for—in breadth or in depth—until we identify our specific needs systematically with the aid of the Mate Map.

For example, from a breadth perspective, we may know that we want someone who is caring, friendly and attractive. However, before we plan to spend the rest of our life with this person, we should also consider a broader range of areas such as religion, age, affection, maturity, jealousy, assertiveness, and responsibility, to name only a few.

From a depth perspective, it's important to determine *specifically* what we are looking for. Let's take a look at an example. (Note that the examples and anecdotes presented in this book are based on the experiences of real people, but names, identifying information and nonessential facts have been changed throughout to protect their privacy. Any similarity to actual individuals is, accordingly, entirely coincidental.)

Patrick, 27, knows in a general way that he prefers women who are career-minded, but he hasn't given the subject much thought. His girlfriend, Marlene, is somewhat of a workaholic who spends long hours on the job and often works on weekends. Therefore he assumes that she is career-minded and that the two of them are an excellent fit in this area. Only after dating for three months does Patrick learn that Marlene eventually wants to have a big family and doesn't feel the need to continue with her career. It took that long to discover this information because Patrick didn't do enough thinking ahead of time about what he specifically wants regarding a mate's career ambition. He simply assumed Marlene was career-minded because of her evident commitment to her job. If Patrick had addressed this subject head-on, he could have had a conversation with Marlene about her level of career ambition sooner rather than later.

Now Patrick has some thinking to do about the extent to which Marlene's lack of career ambition bothers him. Perhaps he'll come to see that it's not especially important to him. Or perhaps he'll realize a mate with strong career ambition is very important to him, accept that he and Marlene are not such a great fit after all, and decide to end the relationship. The point is that Patrick could have avoided investing time, energy and emotion in a relationship that might not be right for him if he had thought more specifically about his wants beforehand.

It is true that once we meet someone, our views about what we want may change. But for the most part we tend to hold on to the beliefs that we bring into a relationship. So, if there are any beliefs that are unclear going into a relationship, they are likely to remain unclear during the relationship. The best way to crystallize our beliefs, either during a relationship or ideally *before* a relationship even begins, is to use the Mate Map.

Once you have completed Phase I of the Mate Map, you will have a valuable pool of information that you can use to shape your relationship future. I refer to this pool of information as your **Ideal Inventory**. Think of your Ideal Inventory as a shopping list of what you want in a mate. This list is something you build over time and can refer to whenever you need it. You'll learn how to create your Ideal Inventory during Phase I of the Mate Map, which is in Chapters 6, 7, 8 and 9.

The second step toward fulfilling our needs is to determine if a specific person is right for us. Whether you're about to go on a first date with someone, or you've already been in a relationship with someone for a while, you can use your Ideal Inventory to help decide whether to start or continue a relationship. By matching your Ideal Inventory to the actual characteristics and behaviors of a potential or current mate, you can determine the extent to which this person meets your needs. You'll learn how to apply your Ideal Inventory starting with Phase II of the Mate Map, which is in Chapter 10.

MATE MAP PRINCIPLE 2
Keep a balance between intuition and rational thinking.

People often expect to know when they have found the right mate because it will just "feel right." Although intuition should play a vital role in deciding who to choose as a mate, rational thinking is needed as well. Too often, people who are typically rational lose their rational perspective when it comes to relationships. When the intuitive side of relationship decision making outweighs the rational side, the relationship falls out of balance. If you rely too much on your intuition, you may not be examining the tangible areas of a relationship that warrant attention. The reverse holds true as well. If you rely too much on rational thinking, you may find yourself with a mate who looks good on paper, but for whom you don't have especially strong feelings. Let's take a look at an example of each of these extremes.

Suzanne, 32, knows she's in love with Josh, 34, her boyfriend of a year. She also knows intuitively that their feelings for each other are genuine. At the same time, Suzanne recognizes that there are some problems in the relationship. For example, Josh doesn't always treat her well. He is sometimes critical of her, which makes her feel inferior. Although this treatment bothers Suzanne, she overlooks these negative aspects because she is so sure of her love for Josh. If Suzanne decides to examine her situation more rationally, she may discover that by letting Josh treat her poorly she is ignoring what she knows is really best for her. Upon this realization she can then try to improve the situation or end the relationship.

Emily, 31, is very excited after going on a few dates with Trent, 30, because he has a lot of what she is looking for in a man—he comes from a good family, he has a good job, he's athletic and he's outgoing. As they continue to date for four months, Emily expects to become more enamored of Trent and fall in love with him. However, this doesn't happen. She is surprised, because it seems to make sense that he is right for her. Holding on to her belief and hoping that she gets bitten by the love bug, Emily continues to date Trent for five more months. Finally she realizes that her feelings for him are simply not deep enough for her to be in a relationship with him, so she breaks up with him.

As you create your Mate Map, you are likely to notice some situations where you tend to favor intuition and others where you tend to favor rational thinking. In order to get the most from the Mate Map system, you should take into account rational as well as intuitive elements for each and every area of a relationship—regardless of which element you tend to favor for a particular area.

MATE MAP PRINCIPLE 3
Examine Personality Fit, Magnetism and Love separately.

When we assess whether someone is right for us, we need to examine three critical areas—Personality Fit, Magnetism and Love. These three areas are what I call the **Relationship Essentials**, or **Essentials** for short. **If we don't have a high level of compatibility with a person for *each* of the Essentials, then this person is not right for us**. Let's take a closer look at each of these terms.

I define **Personality Fit** as the degree of fit between the personality attributes one person desires and the other person possesses. These personality attributes are divided into two groups: the Profile Attributes and the Spectrum Attributes. The **Profile Attributes** are the facts about a person, also known as his or her "stats." Age and religion are examples of Profile Attributes. The **Spectrum Attributes** comprise everything about our personalities from core values and beliefs to specific behaviors.

I define **Magnetism** as the combination of Physical Attraction and Chemistry between two people. **Physical Attraction** is the strong, often passionate attraction that occurs when one person's Physical Attributes match what another person finds desirable. Physical Attributes are simply the aspects of a person's physical appearance. **Chemistry**, the other half of Magnetism, is the natural connection between two people, which includes such intangibles as nonverbal communication and sexual chemistry.

I define **Love** similarly to the way you probably define it— having deep feelings of affection and emotional intensity toward a potential or current mate. This kind of love differs from the love you feel for close friends and family because Love includes the additional elements of intimacy and exclusivity.

On the surface, Personality Fit, Magnetism and Love seem to be quite different from one another. But in the complex world of relationships, these areas are often intertwined, making it difficult or impossible to tell them apart. This leads to a major problem. **If you can't distinguish among the Essentials, then you can't ensure that you are fulfilled in all three areas.** Categorizing the way we think about relationships into Personality Fit, Magnetism and Love allows us to focus on each of these areas separately so we can assess accurately whether a mate fulfills our needs in each area. Here's an example that shows how difficult it can be to tell the Essentials apart.

Leslie, 23, and Jim, 24, met at the party of a mutual friend two months ago. They started talking and hit it off right away. They were only together for twenty minutes, but it was as if they had known each other for twenty years. As the party went on, they mingled separately with friends for a while, but kept glancing at each other from across the room. On one side of the room, Leslie told her friend Shari, "I just talked with this great guy, who is so cute." On the other side of the room, Jim told his friend Larry, "I just had an amazing conversation with that hottie over there."

Later in the evening, Leslie and Jim got together again and chatted for about forty-five minutes. Before Leslie left to go meet a friend at another party, Jim asked for her phone number and she gave it to him. A few days later they went on their first date together.

With their great chemistry and the fact that Leslie found Jim to be very attractive, it is safe to say that Leslie couldn't get enough of Jim. But, five months later, Leslie did have enough of Jim, and she ended things with him. Although her Magnetism with him was high, the Personality Fit was quite low. They had different values, goals, and lifestyles. It's not that Jim's personality had changed at all during these five months, it's that Leslie had treated Magnetism and Personality Fit as one and the same. She assumed that because they had a high level of connection, their personalities were compatible as well. However, over time, as Leslie really got to know Jim, she realized that Magnetism and Personality Fit are actually very different.

Although they are intertwined, the Essentials are not correlated to one another. In other words, it is possible to have a relationship where the more you like your mate's personality, the more physically attracted you become and the deeper you fall in love. But it's also possible to be in a relationship where the extent to which you like your mate's personality increases, but your levels of physical attraction and love remain unchanged. We simply can't rely on one great area of a relationship to cause another area of a relationship to be great. This isn't a situation where you can "borrow" excess greatness from one essential and apply it to another, weaker area. And it is not a "majority wins" situation where just because two out of three Essentials works, the whole thing works. **The only way to have a successful relationship is to make sure that the levels of each of the three Essentials is high.** The following example shows what can happen if you don't examine the Essentials separately.

Diego, 26, is set up, through a mutual friend, on a blind date with Erika, 26. The two of them get along well and continue dating. After their seventh date, Diego decides to figure out if he likes Erika enough to continue a relationship with her.

First, Diego examines the opinions he has formed about Erika. He likes that she is friendly and mellow, but is less than thrilled that at times she can be boring and self-centered. He is physically attracted to her and he thinks their chemistry is amazing. He knows he is not yet in love with her. Diego synthesizes this information in what he feels is a logical way: since he likes four of the six aspects he identified (her friendliness, how mellow she is, her looks and great chemistry), he proceeds to pursue a relationship with Erika.

Although the decision to be with Erika may end up being right or wrong for him, Diego's process in making that decision was faulty. What he should have done was separate each of the factors he thought about into the Relationship Essential categories. What this does is make sure that Diego is thinking about Personality Fit, Magnetism and Love separately.

When the factors are assessed in these terms, Diego's possible future with Erika comes into clearer perspective. It is clear that Love has not been achieved, which is understandable because they have only been dating for a short period of time. It is also clear that there is a high level of Magnetism. However, the level of Personality Fit does not seem to be very high. Diego realizes that Erika can be boring and self-centered, but he really doesn't factor this into his decision. Instead he uses a "majority wins" approach, rationalizing that there are more positives about her than negatives.

What Diego fails to take into account is that, if there isn't a high level of Personality Fit reached at some point, his relationship with Erika is likely to have problems. Even if Diego has a favorable opinion of fifteen of Erika's personality attributes, if there are two other attributes that end up bothering him significantly, then they may not have a high level of Personality Fit as a couple.

Recognizing the Relationship Essentials as separate categories can help Diego to see beyond a strong fit in one of the Essentials (Magnetism), and realize that his relationship with Erika is deficient in the other two Essentials (Personality Fit and Love). Since there is not a strong fit in all three areas, it is unlikely that Diego can have a fulfilling relationship with Erika, and it is in Diego's best interests to no longer pursue a relationship with Erika.

This next example illustrates that we need to be honest with ourselves when assessing Personality Fit, Magnetism and Love.

Irene, 26, recently broke up with her boyfriend, Carl, 27, after going out with him for ten months. When they first met, Irene quickly became interested in Carl. Though at first she did not find him particularly attractive physically, his great personality attracted her to him. As she spent more time with him and got to know him better, Irene fell in love with him. Or so she thought.

After the first six months of the relationship, Irene started feeling that something was missing. She soon realized that she was not attracted to Carl as much as she wanted to be. It's not that she found him unattractive, it's that, based on looks alone, he was not for her. She also realized that, although she did love him, she was not "in" love with him. She cared for him deeply, but it was more like friendship love than romantic love. After a few months of trying unsuccessfully to overcome these problem areas, Irene ended the relationship.

You Control Only You

In order to have a happy and fulfilled relationship, both partners must achieve a high level of Personality Fit, Magnetism
and Love with their mate. However, applying these Relationship Essentials must start with you. The reason is simple—you
can control your own views and opinions, but you cannot
control those of your partner. It's true you can *influence* your
mate's perspective on the Essentials, but you can't *control* it.
Therefore your goal when approaching a potential or current
relationship should be to assess the three Essentials **from
your own perspective**. You want to put yourself in a position
so that, if the Essentials are achieved, you are ready to move
forward in a relationship.

However, if the other person does not know about the Mate
Map, his or her definition of "ready" is probably different from
yours. Your potential mate may want to pursue a relationship
with you, but you don't know if it is for all of the right reasons—
namely, compatibility in the Relationship Essentials. You don't
want to be caught on the receiving end of someone who doesn't
examine your relationship sufficiently and ends up realizing the
two of you are incompatible or your partner is unfulfilled. To
understand the other person's definition of "ready," after you
learn the Mate Map you should introduce him or her to it. You'll
learn how to best go about introducing your potential or current
mate to the Mate Map in Chapter 14, The Ongoing Mate Map.

Next, in Chapter 3, we'll explore Personality Fit. Then, in
the next two chapters, we'll cover Magnetism and Love further,
before you create your own Mate Map.

3

Personality Fit

As I first mentioned in Chapter 2, Personality Fit is defined as the degree of fit between the personality attributes that one person desires and the other person possesses. These personality attributes are divided into two groups: the Profile Attributes and the Spectrum Attributes.

Profile Attributes

I have identified eight attributes that consist of factual information about a person, which I refer to as the Profile Attributes. If you've ever been set up on a blind date, besides finding out about the person's personality and looks ahead of time, you also want to know about this person's "stats." These "stats" are the Profile Attributes. The eight Profile Attributes are: **Age**, **Career/Job**, **Education Level**, **Ethnicity**, **Geographic Desirability**, **Religion**, **Socioeconomic Status**, and **Hobbies/ Interests**. There are examples of each of these Profile Attributes in Chapter 7. These examples provide a full understanding of each attribute, which will be helpful when completing your Mate Map.

Although these eight areas don't necessarily fit our image of what we think of as personality traits, I have included them as a part of Personality Fit, because determining Personality Fit involves using mostly rational thinking to examine attributes. (As opposed to Magnetism and Love, which lean heavily on intuition.)

Most of us want mates with personality attributes similar to our own. This is especially true with the Profile Attributes. And even if we are okay being with someone who has different Profile Attributes than we do, we at least want to know what these Profile Attributes are, so we can examine them and become comfortable with any differences. Besides recognizing current differences, we should think about the long-term as well and do our best to address differences that may emerge over time. Let's take a look at an example.

Scott, 25, and Isabella, 24, have been "boyfriend—girl-friend" for five months before each of them thinks about the possibility of deepening the relationship with a possible eye to marriage. Before they make a decision, they know they need to resolve issues around the fact that they have different ethnic backgrounds and religions. Scott is Caucasian and Lutheran, whereas Isabella is Hispanic and Catholic. They need to get comfortable with the differences themselves, and they also want their families to be comfortable with the differences.

For Scott, the differences are not a big deal. Isabella is every-thing he wants in a mate, and he believes they have all of the right components of a great relationship. It doesn't bother him the slightest bit that her skin color is darker than his is or that they are of different faiths. At first, Scott's parents were con-cerned that the religious difference could cause trouble later on in their relationship. After Scott explains to his parents that he doesn't have any problems with the religion issue and that Isabella makes him happy, they support his decision to move ahead with the relationship.

Isabella, on the other hand, finds the situation more trou-bling. When they first started dating, she was surprised that she was so interested in Scott, since she had always dated Hispanic men and always pictured herself being married to a Hispanic man. Over the five months of their relationship, she became comfortable with the fact that Scott is not Hispanic. It is the beliefs of Isabella's parents that cause her the most anguish. Her parents want their grandchildren to be brought up with certain customs, and they know that Isabella's growing rela-tionship with Scott puts this desire at risk. Although Isabella's parents have met Scott and like him, this doesn't change their opinion that Isabella could just as easily be with someone who is Hispanic and Catholic. Although Isabella is worried about straining her relationship with her parents, she believes Scott is the right one for her, and they decide to deepen their commit-ment to each other. Six months later, Scott and Isabella are very happy together and are talking about getting engaged.

Spectrum Attributes

The second and larger part of Personality Fit is what I call the Spectrum Attributes. The Spectrum Attributes comprise everything about our personalities from core values and beliefs to specific behaviors. These personality traits are termed Spectrum Attributes because each one typifies two personality traits on opposite ends of a spectrum. For example, one of the attributes, **Selfish**, is considered to be at one end of the spectrum, while the opposite attribute, **Unselfish**, is considered to be at the other end. Because our personalities are so complex, there are a countless number of Spectrum Attributes. I have compiled a list of forty-two Spectrum Attributes, which are among the most important to most people. In Chapter 8 you will find examples of each of the forty-two Spectrum Attributes.

The Truths About Personality Fit

Each Essential has particular subtleties that I call the "Truths." By understanding the Truths, you will be able to better apply the Essentials to any dating or relationship situation. There are three Personality Fit Truths, which apply to the Profile and Spectrum Attributes collectively.

PERSONALITY FIT TRUTH I
Our desired attributes are an individual choice.

The Personality Fit each of us wants is different from that of every other person, because there are so many attributes and so many individual desires and needs. It's often the case that an attribute that appeals to one person turns another person off. Although several attributes—such as being kind-hearted and trustworthy—are typically considered desirable, overall,

Personality Fit is based *mostly on personal choice.* It's simply not a good idea to find out what the majority of people desire and then follow the pack. For example, you may meet someone who is quirky in some respect and find this particular attribute to be favorable even though 90% of the population would find such quirkiness a major turnoff. This doesn't mean that there is anything wrong with this person, with you, or with the 10% of the population that would agree with you. It means only that you find a person with this attribute to be a good fit for you.

After getting divorced last year, Janet, 41, is starting to date again. She knows one attribute that is very important to her in a mate is intelligence. As a result, the first question she asks anyone who tries to set her up is, "Is he smart?" When her friend Dean tries to set Janet up with Harvey, 39, a co-worker of Dean's, all Janet needs to hear is that Harvey is smart in order to agree.

However, although Janet likes men who are intelligent, she needs more information regarding Harvey's purported smarts. In the first place, intelligence, along with many other attributes, is relative. Since Janet is a biotechnology engineer with an IQ of 143, her perspective of "intelligence" is different from that of a person with average intelligence, and she must take her own level of intelligence into consideration. Second, she should try to find someone whose level of intelligence fits comfortably with hers. This does not necessarily mean that she needs to find someone whose level of intelligence is equal to hers. Perhaps Janet fits best with a man who is as smart or smarter than she, since she needs a mate who challenges her intellectually. Or perhaps she fits best with someone who is smart enough to have intellectual conversations with, but who is clearly less intelligent than she, as she needs to be intellectually dominant in the relationship.

Ideally, Janet would already know what level of intelligence works best for her before going out with Harvey. If this is the case, once she has determined how intelligent Harvey is, she can easily decide if she wants to continue dating him. If she has not yet figured out the best level of intelligence for her, she should figure it out soon, so that she doesn't waste her time with men who are not right for her.

PERSONALITY FIT TRUTH 2

Be wary of extreme differences and extreme similarities.

Because there are so many personality attributes, it is likely that between any two people there are some attributes where the two people are very similar and others where there are big differences. In some cases, extreme differences may enhance Personality Fit because the couple complements each other. In other cases, extreme similarities can often prevent disagreements. However, we need to be cautious, because sometimes extreme differences or similarities can actually interfere with a good Personality Fit, as the following examples illustrate.

Maggie, 42, and Frank, 43, have been together for three years and currently live together. They get along very well in general, but they often have arguments caused by one extreme difference in their personalities: Maggie is open-minded and trusting, whereas Frank is very critical of others and thinks everyone is incompetent or even dishonest. This difference often surfaces when Maggie and Frank deal with a third party.

This week's argument involves their 18-year-old nephew, Tim, who is staying with them for a few days. When Tim asks Maggie if he can borrow one of their cars to go visit a friend,

Maggie says okay. As Frank walks in the room and sees Maggie handing Tim the car keys, he snatches them away from Tim. He doesn't trust Tim to drive his car, because he remembers that Tim had a minor car accident a year earlier. Maggie is annoyed that Frank is so untrusting and so unforgiving with a member of the family, and Frank is annoyed that Maggie is so overly trusting with someone who cannot be trusted.

Cindy, 20, and Brad, 20, live in the same college dormitory and spend a lot of time together as members of the student government. The positions they hold are Vice President and Treasurer, respectively. When they began to date, Cindy appreciated the many ways in which she and Brad are similar. One of the similarities is that they both have a very high level of leadership. While Cindy likes having a mate who can speak up for himself and take charge of a situation, she also notices that they have difficulty with decision making as a couple, as each person wants to be the one to make final decisions.

Since Cindy is very interested in Brad, she decides that she will try to relinquish some control to him. If she is able to do this, she will then have to assess her comfort level with having less control. If she is either unable to relinquish control, or is not comfortable when she does so, she will have to stop dating Brad and start looking for someone whose attributes of leadership and control do not cause problems for her.

PERSONALITY FIT TRUTH 3
Have "rigid flexibility."

Each of us can probably identify some personality attributes where we will hold out for what we want and identify other attributes where we are flexible. Keeping such a balance is important. From a rigidity standpoint, if you are too rigid you will be making it more difficult to find a mate, not to mention that your rigidity could cause problems in the relationship once you do find someone. This isn't to say that you should settle for just anyone; it's simply that you should be more open-minded. On the other hand, if you are too flexible, your lack of a strong preference might result in choosing someone with whom you don't fit particularly well. Here's an example of an instance when someone was too rigid in his search for Personality Fit.

Ryan, 31, has a very definite picture of what he wants in a mate. He is looking for someone who is between the ages of 25 and 35, is Jewish, very optimistic, full of energy, very witty, intellectual, into spectator sports, and doesn't smoke. And he is not willing to bend on any of these traits. Because of Ryan's narrowly defined list of desired attributes, he may have a hard time finding someone who exactly matches his expectations. And if he does find someone who matches his wish list in these areas, the chances of her being compatible with him in other areas is much less likely. In short, the law of averages works against him.

When Ryan meets Sheryl, a 30-year-old lawyer, at his friend Brett's Super Bowl party, he gets excited. Not only is she the only woman in the room actually watching the game, she also seems to have all of the other qualities he is looking for. But as they go on a few dates and he gets to know her, he becomes less thrilled. She turns out to be messy and unpredictable, whereas he would prefer neatness and predictability. He decides she doesn't have the personality traits he is looking for and stops seeing her.

Over the next six months Ryan has first dates with seventeen different women. Seven of these first dates result in a second date, two of these second dates result in a third date, and none of these third dates result in a fourth date. Suddenly Ryan recognizes how his definitive criteria are preventing him from finding someone. He thinks through what are really the most important areas to him, and decides he's going to be more flexible with his personality attribute wish list. He thinks back to when he met Sheryl and realizes that she is actually what he is looking for, since he can overlook the traits in her personality he finds less than ideal. Ryan calls up his friend Brett to ask if Sheryl is still available. Brett tells him that she has been dating someone for the past three months.

Showing no sympathy for Ryan, Brett says, "You messed up. Sheryl's a great girl. You should have held onto her when you had a chance." All Ryan can do is sigh because he knows that Brett is absolutely right.

4

Magnetism

While Personality Fit accounts for the more rational side of relationships and Love accounts for the more emotional side, Magnetism falls somewhere between the two. Magnetism describes the intangible combination of Physical Attraction and Chemistry.

Physical Attraction

Physical Attraction is the strong, often-passionate attraction that occurs when one person's Physical Attributes match what another person finds desirable.

Most of us could list several Physical Attributes that we look for in a mate. The collection of these traits makes up our "physical type" or simply "type." Having a type is helpful in that we can use it to identify people we're attracted to and to filter out people we're not attracted to. Of the tens of Physical Attributes that are factors in shaping Physical Attraction, I have identified sixteen that are among the most prevalent when determining our type. The sixteen Physical Attributes are: **Hair**, **Eyes**, **Face**, **Smile**, **Lips**, **Teeth**, **Nose**, **Ears**, **Skin**, **Height**, **Body**, **Sex Appeal**, **Cuteness**, **Pretty/Handsome**, **Feminine/Masculine** and **Overall Look**. We will revisit these Physical Attributes in Chapter 9.

Everyone is familiar with the phrase "Beauty is only skin deep," which tells us we should be more concerned with people's inner beauty (personality) than their outer beauty (physical looks). This old saying is true to the extent that our mate's personality should appeal to us in a number of ways, and that it is ultimately more important to us than his or her looks. In fact, we can be led to believe that people who base relationship decisions on Physical Attraction alone are shallow, and that outer beauty is unimportant. However, it's important to keep in mind that Physical Attraction is an internal need, and in itself should not be considered shallow. It is only shallow when we place *too much* emphasis on it in relation to Personality Fit, Chemistry and Love. Besides, Physical Attraction can help to bring two people together. When we meet someone who stirs up our hormones, that feeling is real. Physical Attraction can also help a couple sustain a relationship, by smoothing over the rough edges and serving to deepen their bond. The following example shows how we can benefit by understanding Physical Attraction, even without examining each of the Physical Attributes.

For three years, Len, 44, has been in a relationship with Barbara, 39, and recently they have been talking about getting engaged. Len, who was stressed out from work, decided to take a yoga class where he met Meredith, 28, the yoga instructor. After the class Len approached Meredith to ask her a few questions about yoga, as he was completely new to it. They decided to continue their conversation over a smoothie, during which Meredith became very flirtatious. Len found Meredith to be beautiful, sensual, spiritual and fond of travel, all of which were traits he found appealing. The following week they again shared a smoothie after the yoga class. Afterward, in the parking lot, Meredith invited Len over to her apartment, offering to show him pictures of her trip to New Zealand. Len declined, telling Meredith that he was willing to be friends with her only.

Len knew after their first conversation that Meredith was interested in him, and he suspected she might try to do something about it. So when Meredith invited him over to her place, he already had an answer prepared. His answer was no, but there was a small part of him that wanted to say yes. Len was certainly tempted by Meredith's offer, because never before had such a beautiful woman shown an interest in him. In addition, he and Barbara had been arguing lately. But he declined Meredith's offer and very clearly stated his boundaries to her.

Although Len was never close to saying yes to Meredith's offer, he wanted to understand whether he had simply found her physically attractive, if he just wanted to have one last hurrah before making a more serious commitment to Barbara, or if there were inherent problems in his relationship with Barbara that caused him to consider getting physical with Meredith. So he applied the Relationship Essentials to his situation to figure it out. In his assessment, Len used several important criteria relating to his relationship, including his Personality Fit with Barbara, their Chemistry and Love, as well as the level of his Physical Attraction for both Barbara and Meredith. He realized that his Personality Fit, Chemistry and Love with Meredith were all at a very high level and that there were no major problems in the relationship. Regarding Physical Attraction, Len realized that he still finds Barbara physically attractive after three years of being together. It's true that in the comparison of physical beauty alone, Meredith is more beautiful, but Len realized that his level of Physical Attraction to Barbara is still high.

Len concluded that his Physical Attraction to Meredith was partly because she was a beautiful woman and partly because he was scared about spending the rest of his life being physically intimate with only one woman. Now that he understands the true reasons behind his desires, not only is he more comfortable in knowing that he made the right decision, it also reinforces how special his relationship to Barbara is to him.

Chemistry

Chemistry, the other half of Magnetism, is the natural connection between two people. Whenever we meet someone there is always some level of Chemistry that exists between ourselves and the other person. If we consider the Chemistry to be good or better, we view this person favorably. If the Chemistry is not good, we view this person unfavorably and become uninterested in him or her. After all, why bother spending time with someone with whom we don't particularly click, when there is a whole world full of people with whom we may have better Chemistry?

Although it is often thought that two people either have Chemistry or they don't, Chemistry isn't really so black and white. This is because Chemistry is not just one overall entity, but instead is made up of six different categories. We can have a high level of Chemistry in one category with someone and a low level in another category with that same person. The six **Chemistry Categories** are: **Verbal Communication**, **Nonverbal Communication**, **Sexual Compatibility**, **Desire To Be Together**, **Ease of Getting Along**, and **Influence**. In Chapter 10 these six categories will be covered in more detail.

With the Profile, Spectrum and Physical Attributes, we can arm ourselves fully with the knowledge of what we want in a mate even before dating someone. We can decide what we want so that we can then match it up with the attributes of another person. But with Chemistry we cannot prepare nearly so well, because we are no longer a constant in the equation, as the Chemistry between any two people is unique. In other words, any Chemistry knowledge we gain from one relationship situation cannot be applied to any subsequent relationship with any degree of certainty. For now, let's see how we can best assess Chemistry regardless of this obstacle.

Jill, 26, was excited to go on a blind date with Wayne, 31, after having two great phone conversations with him. Halfway through the date Jill thought to herself, "This guy is amazing." She could already tell they had outstanding Chemistry together. After the date, she decided to put this high level of Chemistry into context. She did this by comparing her Chemistry with Wayne to that of previous men she dated, including two serious relationships she'd had. What she discovered is that her initial level of Chemistry with Wayne was higher than that of anybody else she'd ever dated, even a notch higher than with Steve, her second serious boyfriend. Jill recognizes this is a positive indicator, but she also takes it with a grain of salt, since she recognizes that she has only had one date with Wayne.

The Truths About Magnetism

Just as the three Truths about Personality Fit can give you
insight into that Relationship Essential, so the two Truths
about Magnetism can help you better to understand this
Essential and its difficulties (and rewards).

MAGNETISM TRUTH I
The timeline is irrelevant.

When you hear about Magnetism, you may think it is something that must occur instantly when two people meet, but
this is not necessarily true. Although high levels of either
Physical Attraction or Chemistry *can* happen instantly, that
doesn't mean they *must* happen instantly. Magnetism can be
achieved either instantly or eventually, and one way is not any
better or worse than the other. I refer to this concept as the
"Irrelevant Timeline."

Magnetism may take time to develop for one of two reasons.
First, barriers of circumstance can often prevent two people
from achieving Magnetism. For example, at the time two people meet, one person may be available and the other person
may be in a relationship. Or perhaps one person might be having a bad day or be preoccupied with personal or business matters. In both of these scenarios, external circumstances are
preventing the flow of Magnetism. Second, sometimes two people are simply not wired for instant Magnetism.

As long as there isn't mutual repulsion, it doesn't really
matter whether Magnetism happens instantly, because, as two
people get to know one another, Magnetism can easily
improve. Indeed, the guideline to follow for Magnetism is that

if the levels of Physical Attraction and Chemistry are at least neutral, then you should consider dating this person. If over time the levels do not turn positive, then you should no longer date this person.

The Irrelevant Timeline can often be seen when you look at couples you know. You're likely to find some happy pairs who had instant Magnetism and some who had eventual Magnetism. Here is an example of two couples—one with instant Magnetism and one with eventual Magnetism—who started off differently, but ended up in the same place.

As a FedEx delivery guy, Vince, 23, meets a lot of women on his delivery route. Last year he had a date with a receptionist he met on his route, but it was obvious that the two of them weren't right for each other and there wasn't a second date. Other than that instance, Vince had not found any woman who interested him enough to take out. This changed three months ago when he met Mary, 24, whose company moved into the new office complex on his route. Sparks flew instantly. They went out on a date a few days later, and have been dating ever since.

Rochelle, 28, and Martin, 29, go to the same graduate school, and met when they were assigned to work together on a project. They got along very well but sparks did not fly; their level of Magnetism was neutral. As the semester proceeded and they got to know one another better, their level of Chemistry began to increase. As they learned each other's nuances, they grew closer. Martin started finishing Rochelle's sentences for her. Rochelle playfully retaliated by mimicking the way Martin drinks his coffee, as he always completes his first sip with the same expression of satisfaction—"Aaaahhh . . ." The increase in their Chemistry also led to an increase in Physical Attraction, and one late-night study session turned into a late-night makeout session. Three months after their project started, they began to date.

MAGNETISM TRUTH 2
Don't let yourself be overwhelmed.

A potential problem to be aware of is that a high level of Magnetism can lead to a false sense of confidence. It's easy to think, "it's so good between us that it's bound to be smooth sailing from now on." False confidence in a relationship develops because we become euphoric when we realize that someone we are so drawn to feels the same way about us. It's a feeling that is nearly magical, but it can cloud our judgment. When a couple becomes connected to one another during the early stages of dating, they may believe they have connected on a very high level, but the newness and intensity of their attraction may be giving them a sense of a stronger connection than what actually exists.

To protect yourself from overreacting to Magnetism, always take the newness of the relationship into account, recognizing that part of the wonder of this connection may be the very fact that the relationship is new. Although it's possible that the high level of Magnetism will remain steady or even increase, bear in mind that only time will tell if it will last. Also, you should be cautious so that Magnetism doesn't dominate your relationship. A high level of Magnetism can produce a "halo effect," in which we think everything is right with our new partner, overshadowing the equally important Essentials of Personality Fit and Love.

Shannon, 31, has been in a relationship with Bobby, 30, for one year. Recently, Bobby discussed with Shannon the idea of getting engaged over the next few months. Although

Shannon has been leaning toward getting engaged to Bobby soon, she wants to be sure that Bobby is "the one," so she decides she wants to think about it some more before shopping for an engagement ring. When examining the Essentials, Shannon considers their Magnetism, Personality Fit and Love to be at very high levels. When Shannon tells her sister April, 33, her assessment of how incredible all of the aspects of her relationship with Bobby are, April raises an eyebrow. April has spent a lot of time with both of them, since she and Shannon live together and Bobby often hangs out at their apartment. April agrees that their Magnetism seems to be extremely high, but she does not agree with Shannon's assessment of their degree of Personality Fit and Love.

When Shannon hears April's reaction, she is surprised and a little defensive. She asks April to explain what she means. April points out that, when Shannon talks about how much she loves Bobby, she often mentions superficial elements, such as Bobby's great guitar playing, rather than how much she cares for him. April also tells Shannon that when she and Bobby disagree about something, one of them always changes the subject rather than discussing the dispute. "I'm sorry, Sis," April says, "But to me these are not signs of a couple with a high level of compatibility."

Shannon is at first shocked by April's assessment that both her Personality Fit and Love with Bobby may not be as high as she thinks. Although she hates to admit April may be right, she knows her sister has only her best interests in mind. As a result, Shannon decides not to take any action about getting engaged to Bobby until she has given more thought to their Personality Fit and Love, and can determine if their levels of compatibility in these two areas are nearly as high as their level of Magnetism.

5

Love

When we think about a relationship with a mate, one of the ideas that's in the forefront of our minds is that Love is a mandatory prerequisite for a long-term relationship. This idea is so ingrained within us that we can mistakenly take this belief to mean that, when Love occurs, a great relationship will fall naturally into place. Nevertheless, just because we fall in love, it does not necessarily follow that we will either end up in a relationship with the person we are in Love with *or* that we will be compatible with this person in Personality Fit and Magnetism.

As I first mentioned in Chapter 2, Love is defined as having deep feelings of affection and emotional intensity toward a potential or current mate. Although it is often thought that two people are either in love or they're not, Love isn't really so black and white. This is because Love is not just one overall entity, but instead is made up of six different categories. We can have a high level of Love in one category with someone and a low level of Love in another category with that same person. The six **Love Categories** are: **What You Feel**, **Importance**, **What You Find Special (Or Not Special)**, **Love Fulfillment**, **Love Compatibility**, and **Changes My Outlook For The Better (Or Worse)**. In Chapter 10 these six categories will be covered in more detail.

This definition for Love takes into consideration the feeling of romance as a key emotional difference between *a relationship with a significant other* and *friendships*. This difference is one of the three Truths about Love that we need to recognize in order to build relationships that last.

LOVE TRUTH I
Nonromantic love is different from Relationship Love.

The definition used for Love is appropriate for the type of love I discuss throughout this book, which I call Relationship Love (or simply Love), to distinguish it from the other type of love, which is nonromantic love—the kind we feel for close friends and family. This second type of love differs from Relationship Love in that Relationship Love has a higher level of commitment and intimacy, because we generally open up to our mate more and spend more time with our mate than with family or friends.

When we have a mate, though we typically experience the same sort of nonromantic love we feel toward close friends and family, the additional elements of commitment and intimacy usually transform that nonromantic love into Relationship Love.

Each person in a relationship feels either nonromantic love or Relationship Love, but not both at the same time. You may have heard someone say about her mate, "I love him but I am not *in* love with him." This means that the person does not feel Relationship Love, the type needed for a successful relationship.

Stephanie, 40, and Jay, 45, have been in a relationship for one and a half years. Stephanie is glad that her relationship with Jay has Personality Fit and Magnetism. However, her feelings of love for him are not as intense as she had hoped for. She cares for him very deeply, but more as a best friend than a lover.

Stephanie had recognized a number of months back that something was missing from her relationship, but she could not put her finger on it until now. Having figured out the problem, she is unsure of what to do. On one hand, Jay is an amazing guy to whom she is attracted. On the other hand, she does not love him as intensely as she feels she should if she is going to spend the rest of her life with him. Stephanie decides to keep the relationship going while she tries to determine if she can deepen her love for Jay. Perhaps, she reasons, it is taking her longer to fall in love (or rather "in Love") because she has been hurt in previous relationships. Or perhaps she is simply unable to achieve Relationship Love with Jay, as it is just not there. Whatever answers she finds and whatever decision she makes regarding the relationship, she should concentrate on getting her needs met. And one of those needs is Relationship Love.

LOVE TRUTH 2
We can't control Love.

Just as there are times when we would like to achieve Love with a particular person, there are other times when we fall in

Love with someone we weren't even trying to have a relationship with. Love is a phenomenon whereby an emotional attachment forms and builds, but we can't really control with whom we make this emotional attachment. Sometimes Love just happens. Sure, we can influence Love somewhat by either feeding into it or putting up emotional barriers. However, we can't always choose the person we fall in Love with, which can sometimes lead to difficult or awkward situations.

Drew, 31, first met Linda, 29, ten years ago. At that time, Drew's best friend, Allan, had a big summer bash at his house before they went their separate ways and returned to their respective colleges for their senior year. It was at this party that Drew met Linda, Allan's girlfriend. Drew found her to be nice, but at the time really thought nothing in particular about their meeting. Drew had seen Linda several more times subsequently, as Allan and Linda continued to go out for two more years. Shortly after Allan and Linda broke up, Linda moved to another town a thousand miles away and lived there for seven years. Then, a year ago, Linda moved back to the town where she grew up, which is where Drew and Allan, still best friends, still lived. Coincidentally, Linda rented an apartment in Drew's apartment complex. One day they ran into each other at their local supermarket. After the initial surprise of seeing each other for the first time in seven years, they discovered that they both worked in the same office complex. They decided to commute to work together, and over the course of eight months they fell in Love.

After Drew first ran into Linda, he mentioned it to Allan. However, while Drew was falling in Love with Linda, he didn't mention it to Allan. The reason was that he felt somewhat uncomfortable about the situation and he didn't want his relationship with Linda to affect his relationship with Allan.

Although Drew knew that Allan would be happy for him, Drew was concerned that Allan would also have difficulty with the fact that his best friend was now in a relationship with the first woman Allan was ever in Love with. "I can't believe it," Drew said. "Out of all the millions of women, I fall in love with my best friend's ex-girlfriend?" Believe it, Drew. It happens.

Our lack of control over Love can also lead us to fall in Love with people who may not be right for us. It is so important—and difficult—to recognize this concept; however, unless we do, we can easily find ourselves in a relationship that is not good for us. Remember: Love is only one of the three Relationship Essentials that are crucial for a great relationship. No matter how incredible your level of Love, it cannot compensate for a lack of Personality Fit or Magnetism.

Kyle, 24, and Tina, 22, are in Love. They met two years ago when Kyle went into the store where Tina was working to pick up a birthday present he had ordered for his girlfriend at the time. Kyle was floored the first time he met Tina. He found her to be charming, witty and very cute. As a result, he could not stop thinking about her, and began to stop by the store often to talk to her. He could tell that Tina liked him also, so he asked her out on a date, and she accepted. They had a wonderful time together. Kyle then broke up with his girlfriend, as he liked Tina so much more.

After being together for seven months, the couple starts to have problems. Despite their amazing levels of Magnetism and Love, their Personality Fit is not good at all. They have continual arguments that are more than basic disagreements. Their outlooks on life are very different, and the conflicts that result are starting to take a toll on their relationship. During the past year they have been trying to work out their problems, but have made little progress. Kyle still loves Tina, but the relationship is not working, and sooner or later he will have to face the reality that the relationship must end.

LOVE TRUTH 3
Love works best when we fall in Love at a natural pace.

So how can we avoid falling in Love with someone who is not good for us? We should consider slowing down the pace of falling in Love. In other words, we should learn to let it happen or not happen naturally, without inflaming it with our fantasies and projections. Let's face it: we are all in love with the *idea* of falling in Love, because Love is wonderful. But there is a negative aspect to Love as well. The great feelings we experience when we're in Love also cloud our judgment. When we are in the midst of falling in Love, we tend to see all of the positive aspects of the loved one, but not the negative aspects. But if the couple turns out to be truly incompatible, then the deep level of Love will make it much more difficult to end the relationship, and leave both individuals more deeply hurt. As we can see from this example, force-feeding Love can lead to a negative outcome that could have been avoided.

After dating casually for three months, Patty, 25, and Chris, 28, fall in Love. Patty is brimming with excitement, since this is the first time she has been in Love. Her feelings for her three previous boyfriends never evolved into Love. With Chris, she is certain that her deep emotional feelings are real. When her friend raves about the Mate Map, Patty gives it a try. She suddenly realizes that Love is the only strong part of their relationship. There are several areas of Personality Fit and Magnetism where they are not a match. Patty is taken aback upon this realization, but once she sees it on paper and thinks about it more, she realizes it is true. It quickly becomes clear to her that Chris is not right for her.

At first, Patty has a difficult time comprehending how she could fall in Love with someone who is incompatible with her in so many areas. Eventually she realizes the reason is that she wanted to be in Love so badly, and was *looking* to fall in Love with him. Yes, her Love for Chris is true, but had she not tried so hard to be in Love with him, she believes she would have realized their mismatches and not fallen in Love with him. Instead, she is about to face a painful break-up.

TWO

The Mate Map:
Phase 1—Ideal Inventory

6

Mapping the Relationship Essentials

Here you will begin creating your own personal Mate Map. Starting in Phase I, you will create your Ideal Inventory by identifying and prioritizing the Profile, Spectrum and Physical Attributes that are most important to you. In Phases II, III, IV and V, you will apply your Ideal Inventory to a particular person. If you're single, the person can be anyone with whom you've been on one or more dates. If you're currently in a relationship, the person would be your mate. If you're not dating anyone right now, you'll learn what to do for when you are dating someone.

As you go from Phase I through Phase V, you will find exercises labeled Section A through Section G. With each exercise are simple step-by-step instructions, examples of a completed exercise form and a blank exercise form.

The Power of the Pen

Relationships are nebulous and complex, making it difficult to wrap our minds around them. To get a better understanding of what you're really feeling and thinking about relationships in general, or a given relationship, it's extremely helpful to put down your thoughts in writing when completing the Mate Map exercises. Your initial reaction may be a groan, but I assure you that this process will prove to be worthwhile. Getting used to writing your thoughts down will not take long at all. Remember, it also felt strange the first few times you walked down the street talking on a mobile phone and it appeared to others around you that you were talking to yourself. Now you probably don't think twice about it.

The reason it's necessary to write down information about a relationship is that . . . it works! We learn best when we write. In fact, from the mid-1970s through the new millennium, the idea of "learning through writing" has been gaining favor in a number of fields. In education, it's called "Writing Across the Curriculum." Universities and high schools across the country have been implementing this program, which emphasizes writing in all aspects of the learning process. Educational institutions have found that writing helps people to think, probe ideas, make connections, organize thoughts, retain information, and understand any subject matter more thoroughly than reading or thinking alone. Furthermore, writing encourages revision, literally "re-seeing," which prevents us from locking into an idea that may need to evolve.

The participants in the Mate Map Study found the written exercises to be vital to the Mate Map process. Comments included, "The exercises enabled me to focus on my relationship and my needs" and "It is important to write down your thoughts. By answering some of the questions it helps you clear some things in your head."

The Exercise Forms Are Unlimited

Most of the blank exercise forms within each Section provide you room to map one attribute per form. But since you will be mapping multiple attributes, additional forms are needed. You can get these additional forms for free at **www.matemap.com**. Just click on the area called "**Exercise Forms**" and follow the simple instructions to get your 8 ½" x 11" forms. You will be able to print out as many exercise forms as you like.

Many people prefer not to write in the book at all and only use the forms found at the website. Others prefer to write in the book initially and then go online when they need additional forms. Choose whichever of these ways you are more comfortable with.

If this is a library book or you are borrowing this copy from a friend, please **DO NOT WRITE IN IT**. Instead, go to www.matemap.com and print out your own exercise forms. If you don't have access to the internet, or don't have a printer, you can photocopy the exercise forms in Appendix B. Before you continue to the next chapter, Chapter 7, you may want to go to www.matemap.com and print out the exercise forms, so that you will have them on hand when you are ready to start mapping.

Now or Later

I recommend doing the exercises as you go through each chapter. However, if you decide to read through the chapters and then go back to do the exercises later, that's okay too. Just make sure that you complete all of the exercises within one Phase before continuing to the next Phase.

And now, it's time to start mapping.

7

The Profile Attributes

The first part of your Ideal Inventory will be created by examining the Profile Attributes. Before you map the Profile Attributes, let's take a closer look at each of them. As first listed in Chapter 3, the eight Profile Attributes are: Age, Career/Job, Education Level, Ethnicity, Geographic Desirability, Religion, Socioeconomic Status, and Hobbies/Interests. In the pages that follow, the Profile Attributes are listed alphabetically, along with examples of how incompatibilities within them can cause problems. Even if an example is not immediately relevant to you, it should stimulate thinking to help you identify how each attribute might apply to you.

Age

Robin, 36, is in a relationship with Andre, 26. Andre has no problem with the fact that Robin is ten years older than he is. Although Robin does like Andre very much, and thinks she may be falling in Love with him, she is somewhat unsettled because she is with a man who is much younger than she is. All Robin's past relationships were with men at least three years older than she was, so that's what she's used to. Robin needs to decide whether the age difference is just another thing she needs to get accustomed to, or is something that will continue to bother her.

Career/Job

Eric, 45, and Nora, 43, have been in a relationship for two years. Previously, Eric's first wife passed away and Nora's first marriage ended in divorce. After being a nurse for eighteen years, Nora decides that she wants to change careers and open a boutique that sells women's clothing. Eric is usually supportive of Nora's endeavors, but he doesn't support her in this career change. When he was dating Nora, he admired her for being in a profession where she could make a real difference in society. He simply doesn't respect her new plans as much as her nursing career.

Education Level

Deena, 31, and Will, 33, have been on six dates and they like each other a lot. On their sixth date, Will tells a story during which the following words come out of his mouth: ". . . and then when I dropped out of college . . ." After Will finishes his story, Deena asks him, "So when did you go back and get your degree?" Will tells her he never finished college, and her jaw drops. When Will sees her reaction, he asks, "Oh, does that bother you?" "Of course not!" Deena exclaims. "I just assumed you were a college graduate."

But the truth of the matter is that Will's failure to get a degree bothers Deena a lot. She is a teacher, with a master's degree in education, and her father, mother and brother all have graduate degrees. It is safe to say that Deena values education highly. On the other hand, she hasn't liked someone as much as Will in a long time. And he does have a really good job now. So the question she has to ask herself is, "Does it really matter that he doesn't have a college degree?"

Ethnicity

Larry, 26, has been single for the past year, as he hasn't found anyone he likes enough to have a relationship with. His last girlfriend, Aleisha, 25, was much like all the other girls he dated—African American, energetic, and petite. Although he only had one real relationship with any of these women—his six-month relationship with Aleisha—he still found these three attributes very appealing to him.

One day the consulting firm Larry works for assigns him to a telecommunications company, where he starts working on a project with one of their employees, Sara, 25. After working with Sara for a week, Larry realizes he is physically attracted to her and likes her personality. This catches him completely off guard, since Sara is Korean, and he has never been attracted to an Asian woman before.

Larry decides he wants to understand his attraction to Sara better. Using the Mate Map, Larry recognizes that Sara is both energetic and petite, and actually fits many of the other traits he liked in his previous experiences with women. Further reflection leads Larry to realize he never previously dated Asian women because he incorrectly stereotyped them as being demure and withdrawn, which is in contrast to his desire to find someone who is energetic. Now he realizes this stereotype is not necessarily true, and it's opening up a whole new world to him.

Geographic Desirability

Heather, 31, and Andrew, 33, have been in a relationship for the past year in their hometown of Cincinnati. The packaging company where Andrew has worked for five years has announced a restructuring. The good news is that Andrew is being promoted, and in one year he could possibly be promoted again. The bad news is that his new position is in the company's Denver location, 1,200 miles away. He is told, however, that after being in Denver for a year he can be transferred back to the Cincinnati location.

Andrew thinks through his options. He could stay in Cincinnati with Heather, but, not only would he be giving up a job he loves, the economy has been declining and he doesn't like his chances of finding another good job in Cincinnati. He could have Heather move to Denver with him, but he doesn't think she wants to leave, because she is very close to her family and also helps run the family business. He could move to Denver without Heather, since it would only be for a year, and he would be able to see her for one week out of every month when he's in Cincinnati to conduct monthly training sessions at his former location. Andrew and Heather agree that this third option is the best of the three. They are determined not to let the distance come between them, despite the hardship of being apart for so long.

Religion

Renee, 24, and Evan, 24, have been dating for three months. Renee is Jewish and likes the fact that Evan is Jewish also. However, Evan is much more religious than Renee is, and obeys the Sabbath from Friday at sundown to Saturday at sundown. During this holy day of rest, Evan goes to temple twice and doesn't go out socializing. This bothers Renee, because at the end of the work-week she likes to go out on the town and have fun. It's true that she occasionally enjoys Friday night dinners at home with Evan and his family—but not every single Friday night. Renee realizes that this very important difference in her and Evan's fundamental beliefs may indicate that they are not right for each other.

Socioeconomic Status

Todd, 28, and Paige, 26, have been dating for two months. Todd has always had money in his family, whereas Paige is from a middle-class family that at times struggled financially. Tension begins to build when the couple realizes that they have very different approaches to money. Todd is extremely concerned with money, viewing it as a source of power. Paige has little interest in money, as she needs just enough money to buy some basic things. After a few discussions aimed at trying to understand each other's viewpoint, Todd and Paige fail to resolve the issue. They mutually agree they are not a good fit for each other and stop dating.

Hobbies/Interests

Tamara, 25, and Brad, 30, met at a softball game. They were on opposing teams and caught each other's eye. When Tamara got a single in the third inning, she ended up on first base, which is the position Brad was playing. They flirted for a few minutes until the inning ended. After the game, when both teams went out for drinks, they met up again and started talking. Besides their obvious common interest in softball, Tamara discovered that they both enjoy playing tennis, eating sushi, reading biographies, and watching independent films. Tamara is excited to find someone who shares the same hobbies and hopes that Brad asks her out on a date. Her excitement gets curtailed when Brad says, "Do you like dogs? I love dogs. I've got two huskies named . . ." As Brad continues talking about his dogs, Tamara thinks to herself, "Ugh!" She hates dogs. Not only is she extremely allergic to them, she was once bitten by a neighbor's dog and has a scar to show for it. All of sudden she's not so sure she would go on a date with Brad after all.

Mapping Instructions for Section A1

Here you will begin creating your Ideal Inventory. These instructions refer to Form 1 on Page 72.

Description

All Section A exercises relate to the Profile Attributes. In Section A1 you will choose how important each of the Profile Attributes is to you. The first column to the far left is labeled

Attribute No. You can use this number as a reference point as you go through your Mate Map. The second column lists page numbers for easy reference to the examples in this chapter. The third column is a list of Profile Attributes. To the right of the Profile Attributes is the four-point scale of importance. The choices are: **Extremely Important**, **Very Important**, **Moderately Important** and **Slightly Important**. This scale allows you to rate how important each Profile Attribute is to you, relative to the other Profile Attributes.

Instructions

Read through these instructions once, then read them again as you complete Form 1 on Page 72.

Starting with the first Profile Attribute, **Age**, place a checkmark in the box to the right that best describes how important that Profile Attribute is to you. Then continue down the page until you have placed one checkmark in each row where there is a Profile Attribute listed. As you consider each Profile Attribute, keep in mind you should also be thinking about how important this attribute is to you relative to the other Profile Attributes.

The purpose of identifying the level of importance for each attribute is to help you focus on the ones that are most important to you and pay less attention to the ones you deem less important. To better understand each Profile Attribute, you may want to refer back to the examples, which begin on Page 62.

You'll notice that, below the eight Profile Attributes listed, there are spaces for two additional attributes. If you come up with any additional attributes on your own and want to map them, simply write your new Profile Attributes in the appropriate blank spaces on Form 1 and determine the level of importance for each. It's helpful to keep in mind that the Mate Map is a complete system that can be used as is *or* can be can be adjusted to suit your needs.

If, in reviewing the list of Profile Attributes, you find a large number of attributes you consider Extremely Important, you should not mark all of them with this designation. The purpose of Mate Mapping is to prioritize what is truly most important to you. Remember that in any dating or relationship situation you will need to make compromises regarding what you are looking for and how the other person fits what you are looking for. By choosing all the attributes as Extremely Important, you would not be giving yourself the flexibility to make any compromises.

On Page 72 is a blank Section A1 form for you to use (Form 1). You can also print out a copy of Form 1 from www.matemap.com by clicking on "Exercise Forms" and following the simple instructions. Alternatively, you can photocopy Form 1 from Appendix B.

Go ahead now and return to the beginning of this section, referring to the instructions as you complete Section A1.

Mapping Instructions for Section A2

The best way to understand how to complete Section A2 is to use an example. The example we will use is for the Profile Attribute **Age**, which is on Page 73.

Instructions

Read through these instructions once, then read them again as you complete Form 2 on Page 75. Follow the same steps for any Profile Attributes that you map beyond your first one.

Step 1

Review the importance ratings of the Profile Attributes you mapped in Section A1 and choose the one in the Extremely Important category that is the most important to you. Write this attribute in the blank space provided. If you have difficulty determining which attribute is most important, then choose any of those rated Extremely Important. If you haven't marked any attribute as Extremely Important, then choose the attribute that is most important to you among those you deemed to be Very Important. In the example, Debbie, a 29-year-old graphic designer, chooses Age and writes "Age" on the blank line.

Step 2

Copy your importance rating from Section A1 into the appropriate box. In the example, Debbie places a checkmark in the box next to Extremely Important.

Step 3

With regard to this attribute, write in what you are ideally looking for and not looking for in a mate. Be as specific as possible. In the example, Debbie writes, "I'm looking for someone who is 30 to 35 years old."

Step 4

List the reasons that explain why you are looking for the particular trait. In the example, Debbie writes in two reasons: "I find that I relate better to people around my age. Also, men who are at least 30 tend to be more mature." Although it's not an explicit part of this example, people who have used the Mate Map have found it helpful to think about experiences from past relationships (regardless of whether they are positive or negative) when rating an attribute.

Step 5

Rate your flexibility with regard to this attribute, using the five-point scale. The choices are: **Not Flexible (Dealbreaker)**, **Slightly Flexible**, **Moderately Flexible**, **Very Flexible** and **Extremely Flexible**. In the example, Debbie places a checkmark in the box next to Moderately Flexible. This means that when she meets a man she is interested in, if he is younger than 30 years or older than 35, she may not view the issue of Age as a problem. For example, being Moderately Flexible and 29 years old, Debbie will likely date a 28-year-old but not a 24-year-old. However, of course she is unable to make an absolute determination until she can apply her Moderate Flexibility to an actual dating situation.

The importance of selecting your level of flexibility is that it creates a benchmark from which to base your decisions. This way, when you meet someone you are interested in, you'll already know the attributes you are willing to compromise on, as well as those that are absolute.

Another example from Debbie's Mate Map can be found on Page 74. This example is for the Profile Attribute **Education Level**.

On Page 75 is a blank Section A2 form for you to use (Form 2). When you have completed it, you can choose either to continue mapping other Profile Attributes or proceed to the next section. If you choose to map more attributes now, go to www.matemap.com, click on "Exercise Forms," and print out as many copies of Form 2 as you need. Alternatively, you can photocopy Form 2 from Appendix B. If you choose to continue to the next section, you can go back to map other Profile Attributes later. Remember, the more attributes you map, the better you'll understand what you are looking for and the better prepared you'll be to make the best relationship decisions for yourself.

Go ahead now and return to the beginning of this section, referring to the instructions as you complete Section A2.

Section A1

Form I

Make a checkmark in one of the four boxes across
to identify the relative importance of each attribute to you.

Attribute No.	Page No.	Profile Attributes	Extremely Important	Very Important	Moderately Important	Slightly Important
1	62	Age				
2	62	Career/Job				
3	62	Education Level				
4	63	Ethnicity				
5	64	Geographic Desirability				
6	65	Religion				
7	65	Socioeconomic Status				
8	66	Hobbies/Interests				
(Add one)						
(Add one)						

Section A2

Example 1

Step 1

Write in an attribute you determined to be of high importance in Section A1.

Profile Attribute 1

Age

Step 2

How important is this attribute to you?

Extremely Important	✓
Very Important	
Moderately Important	
Slightly Important	

Step 3

Ideally, what are you looking for (and not looking for)?

I'm looking for someone who is 30 to 35 years old.

Step 4

What are the reasons for your preference?

I find that I relate better to people around my age. Also, men who are at least 30 tend to be more mature.

Step 5

How flexible are you about your ideal?

Not Flexible (Dealbreaker)	
Slightly Flexible	
Moderately Flexible	✓
Very Flexible	
Extremely Flexible	

Section A2

Example 2

<table>
<tr>
<td>Step 1</td>
<td>Write in an attribute you determined to be of high importance in Section A1.</td>
<td>Profile Attribute 2

Education Level</td>
</tr>
</table>

<table>
<tr>
<td rowspan="4">Step 2</td>
<td rowspan="4">How important is this attribute to you?</td>
<td>Extremely Important</td>
<td></td>
</tr>
<tr>
<td>Very Important</td>
<td>✓</td>
</tr>
<tr>
<td>Moderately Important</td>
<td></td>
</tr>
<tr>
<td>Slightly Important</td>
<td></td>
</tr>
</table>

<table>
<tr>
<td>Step 3</td>
<td>Ideally, what are you looking for (and not looking for)?</td>
<td>Someone who has a college degree.</td>
</tr>
</table>

<table>
<tr>
<td>Step 4</td>
<td>What are the reasons for your preference?</td>
<td>I have a college degree and I want my mate to have one also, because I want both of us to be well educated.</td>
</tr>
</table>

<table>
<tr>
<td rowspan="5">Step 5</td>
<td rowspan="5">How flexible are you about your ideal?</td>
<td>Not Flexible   (Dealbreaker)</td>
<td></td>
</tr>
<tr>
<td>Slightly Flexible</td>
<td>✓</td>
</tr>
<tr>
<td>Moderately Flexible</td>
<td></td>
</tr>
<tr>
<td>Very Flexible</td>
<td></td>
</tr>
<tr>
<td>Extremely Flexible</td>
<td></td>
</tr>
</table>

Section A2

Form 2

Step 1

Write in an attribute you determined to be of high importance in Section A1.

Profile Attribute 1

_____

Step 2

How important is this attribute to you?

Extremely Important	
Very Important	
Moderately Important	
Slightly Important	

Step 3

Ideally, what are you looking for (and not looking for)?

Step 4

What are the reasons for your preference?

Step 5

How flexible are you about your ideal?

Not Flexible (Dealbreaker)	
Slightly Flexible	
Moderately Flexible	
Very Flexible	
Extremely Flexible	

8

The Spectrum Attributes

The second and largest part of your Ideal Inventory will be created by examining the Spectrum Attributes. Before you map the Spectrum Attributes, let's take a closer look at each of them. As I mentioned in Chapter 3, I have identified forty-two Spectrum Attributes, which seem to be among the most important to most people. Examples for each are given in this chapter. Of the forty-two Spectrum Attributes listed, there are certain to be some that are Extremely Important to you, while others will only be Slightly Important to you. In addition there may be other Spectrum Attributes that are important to you but are not on the list. If so, you will have the opportunity to add these to your Mate Map.

Note that the two attributes that make up each Spectrum Attribute are intended to be opposites. However, since words and phrases often have multiple meanings, it is difficult if not impossible for the attributes at the ends of each spectrum to be definitive opposites. For example, if one end of a spectrum is **Down-To-Earth**, then what is the opposite attribute? One person may believe the opposite meaning is **Flighty**, whereas another person may believe it to be **Pretentious**. Both may be correct, depending on which definition of Down-To-Earth is used. If you encounter any Spectrum Attributes you'd like to change, feel free to do so.

When mapping the Spectrum Attributes, you'll find some pairs of attributes in which one is commonly held to be desirable, while the other is traditionally viewed as undesirable. There are other sets of attributes where the desired attribute is just as clearly a matter of personal preference. For example, most people would agree that being Trustworthy is preferable to being Untrustworthy, whereas one person may prefer someone who is Energetic and another person may prefer someone who is Mellow.

Bear in mind that some listed attributes may not technically be personality traits, but are included because they are more relevant to the rational thinking involved with Personality Fit than the more intuitive areas of Chemistry and Love.

The Two Truths About Mapping the Spectrum Attributes

Before you read through the list and examples of the Spectrum Attributes and complete Section B of your Mate Map, you should consider these two Truths about mapping the Spectrum Attributes.

MAPPING THE SPECTRUM ATTRIBUTES TRUTH I
Get as complete a picture as possible.

For purposes of mapping, think of your mate as an entity composed of many different Spectrum Attributes. In order to know how well you fit with this person, you'll need to examine enough of those attributes to get a complete picture. You needn't examine all forty-two of the listed attributes, because some will be either unimportant or irrelevant to you. But you should examine enough attributes to be confident that your personalities mesh well—or to notice that there are potential major problems in the fit. Although you will only map one attribute as you go through this chapter, I recommend that you eventually examine at least twenty-five Spectrum Attributes to get a comprehensive picture.

Laura, 27, has been casually dating Kevin, 27, for three months. After they have a talk about being exclusive, Laura decides to examine the relationship using the Mate Map, because she wants to make sure there is an appropriate Personality Fit. She identifies seven areas where she and Kevin have an excellent or very good Personality Fit. For example, she finds that he's Calm, he's Sociable, he's Not Jealous, he's Relaxed, he's Mature, he's Affectionate and he's Sincere, all of which meet her desires. However, Laura identifies two areas where there is a fair or poor Personality Fit—Kevin's Indecisive and he's a Spender. Laura thinks that these two problems are not crucial and may get better, so she agrees to become exclusive with Kevin.

Six months later, problems emerge when Laura realizes there are more than two areas where her fit with Kevin is not good. She has come to see that Kevin is Selfish and Demanding. In retrospect, she realizes there were faint glimpses of these traits when they were first dating. These two attributes somehow slipped through the cracks, since she never examined them using the Mate Map. She decides to reevaluate the relationship by addressing these and other problematic traits that she didn't examine the first time.

MAPPING THE SPECTRUM ATTRIBUTES TRUTH 2
A rotten few can spoil the bunch.

Personality Fit stands out from the other two Essentials because it contains a far greater number of elements. Although the large number of Spectrum Attributes provides us with the ability for our personality to mesh with our mate's personality in many areas, there are still many areas where a poor fit can still undermine the relationship. Thus, no matter how great the fit in compatible areas, it's critical to identify attributes that have the potential to cause problems.

Matthew, 30, and Courtney, 30, have been together for seven months. However, this is not an entirely new relationship, as five years earlier they went out for two years. For the first year and a half of "Part I" of their relationship, their personalities were highly compatible. But over the next six months their Personality Fit declined, which led to the breakup. The decline happened mostly because of two problems they could not overcome. Matthew found that when something was bothering Courtney, she didn't say anything about it until they were in the middle of a fight. For her part, Courtney felt that Matthew wouldn't listen to any suggestions she made, and he behaved as if everything she said was unimportant. They tried hard to make the relationship work, but were unsuccessful, so they agreed to break up and remain friends.

Now for Part II of their relationship: Matthew and Courtney think their relationship will work this time, because they each admit to having behaved badly in the past. Furthermore, they have each used the Mate Map to pinpoint any new problems they need to be mindful of. People change, and in the process Personality Fit changes as well. While the jury is still out on whether Matthew and Courtney will stay together, they're working systematically to restore their original high level of Personality Fit.

List and Examples of the Spectrum Attributes

Following are the forty-two Spectrum Attributes, listed alphabetically, along with examples of each to help you to recognize them. Even if an example is not relevant to you, it should stimulate thinking in regard to that attribute.

Able to Relax—Uptight

Elaine, 27, and Tom, 29, are both excited about their upcoming four-day weekend together. Since they are saving for a big vacation sometime in the future, they decide to lounge around locally.

On their first day off, a Thursday, they decide to sit by the pool at Elaine's parents' house, which is in a nearby town. Within an hour of arriving, Tom calls his office to check on the status of a project. After the twenty-minute phone call ends, Elaine comments, "I thought you wanted to relax today." Tom replies, "I do. I just need to take care of a few things." He then proceeds to make another call to the office that lasts nearly an hour.

After lunch, Tom and Elaine discuss plans to go boating the next day. Tom expresses a concern that the weather may not be ideal, so perhaps they shouldn't go. Elaine responds, "It's supposed to be nice out tomorrow. If it's a little more cloudy or windy than we'd like it to be, we'll deal with it." She then asks him why he's been so uptight lately. Tom says, "I'm just stressed about work and it still affects me even though I'm not at the office." He then promises to relax the rest of the weekend. Tom is in fact able to relax for the remainder of the weekend, but Elaine is concerned that he seems to have so much trouble letting go of business matters during his leisure time.

Adaptable—Unadaptable

Pamela, 36, plans a nice romantic weekend away at a bed-and-breakfast with her boyfriend Barry, 41. On Wednesday, two days before they are about to leave for their weekend getaway, Barry asks Pamela if they can postpone their plans. The reason is that Barry's college roommate, Don, 41, whom Barry hasn't seen in two years, is coming into town that same weekend, and Barry wants to spend time with him. Although slightly upset at first, Pamela understands that this is a unique situation and agrees to reschedule the trip for another weekend. Barry is appreciative of Pamela's adaptability.

Affectionate—Not Affectionate

Enrique, 34, and Pilar, 33, have been in a relationship for two years. When they are out in public, Pilar frequently reaches out to hold Enrique's hand or put her arm around him. Enrique usually pulls away. When Pilar asks Enrique about this reaction, he tells her that he simply isn't comfortable with public displays of affection. However, she notices that he tends to pull away when they are in private as well, except when sex is in the offing. She sadly concludes that he is near the "Not Affectionate" end of the Affectionate–Not Affectionate spectrum.

Assertive—Unassertive

Brian, 24, and Tanya, 22, have been dating for three months. One day at Wal-Mart, Tanya waits in the checkout line while Brian browses a magazine nearby. He sees that Tanya is about to be the next person called to the register, so he puts away the magazine he's looking at and goes to join her. "What's taking so long?" he asks.

Tanya whispers, "That guy [she points to the man standing at the register] just cut in front of me." "So what happened when you said something to him?" Brian asks. When Tanya explains that she didn't say anything to the man, Brian is flabbergasted. "Why didn't you say anything?" he demands.

Tanya shrugs. "I didn't want to make a scene," she says. Brian lets it go, but he will keep a watchful eye on her level of assertiveness, since he believes strongly that women should stick up for themselves. His mother always lets people walk all over her, and it bothers him greatly. He doesn't want a mate who is unassertive as well.

Calm—Hotheaded

On their fourth date, Nicole, 28, and Roy, 28, dine at an expensive French restaurant, where they encounter several problems. When the couple arrives, they have to wait twenty minutes for a table, even though they had a reservation. And, once they are seated, Nicole notices a vent is blowing cold air directly on her. They call the waiter over and ask him politely to lower the air conditioning, which he agrees to do. Ten minutes later, Nicole is still shivering from the air conditioning.

Roy approaches the maitre d' and sternly explains the situation, again asking for the problem to be taken care of. Within five minutes the air conditioning is lowered, and Roy and Nicole review the menu. When the waiter comes over to take their order, Roy, unable to pronounce the French words on the menu, says, "She'll have the chicken special and I'll have the steak special." The waiter responds that they are out of both dishes. Roy raises his voice and tells the waiter that he should have told them they were out of certain specials earlier. When the waiter simply shrugs, Roy's face turns red and he starts ranting about the terrible service. Nicole interjects, saying, "We'll just order something else."

Though Roy says he's calmed down from his tirade, his mood is obviously still affected during dinner, and then later when they go to a bar. Nicole is concerned about Roy's apparent inability to get over his rage. She is calm and level-headed herself, and doesn't want to be with someone who cannot control his anger.

Compromises—Doesn't Compromise

Valerie, 38, and Adam, 41, have been going out for eight months when they decide to plan a week-long vacation together. Valerie says she would like to go to Europe, since she is interested in history, art, and architecture. Adam, who has a high-pressure job as a managing director at a large investment bank, wants to spend his time off relaxing on a Mexican beach. He has no desire to travel around Europe since he travels all the time and wants to stay in one place. Valerie realizes that they need to compromise, and suggests they find a way to meet both their needs, such as going on a Mediterranean cruise.

Adam, however, balks. "I work my tail off for 70 hours a week," he proclaims. "I don't want to do anything but sit on a beach and drink frozen margaritas." Valerie empathizes with Adam and is considering giving in to his wishes. However, Valerie is not sure she should give in. After all, he should understand that she has needs also.

Decisive—Indecisive

Danny, 35, has always wanted a boat, and now he can afford to buy one, albeit a used one. His girlfriend Tara, 32, is excited for his sake, and also because she looks forward to inviting other couples to go boating with them.

Danny looks through the classified ads and finds five boats in his price range. He goes to see each boat and, of these, finds two he likes a lot. Both are in excellent condition, have 220-horsepower engines and have seating for eight—his top three requirements beyond price. But there are some differences between the two boats. For example, one has newer and more accurate measuring equipment, while the other one has a higher-quality engine. As Danny examines the pros and cons of each boat, he keeps going back and forth between which one he wants more. After a week and a half, he makes a decision and calls the current owner of the boat to make an offer. The owner tells Danny that the boat has already been sold. Although he's disappointed, Danny is fine moving to his second choice. However, this boat too had already been sold while Danny was busy contemplating his decision.

When Tara asks Danny, "So, which boat did you get?" he explains what happened. She just stands and shakes her head in disbelief. This is not the first time that Danny's indecisiveness has left him "missing the boat."

Disciplined—Has No Self-Control

When Lynn, 28, finds out that her cholesterol is 270, well above the acceptable ceiling of 200, she knows she has to alter her diet. Her doctor tells her to eliminate fatty foods, including red meat, fried foods, and most sweets. Two weeks later, Lynn's boyfriend Victor, 29, comes over to her apartment and finds two packages of Oreos in her cabinet. He says, "You aren't supposed to be eating cookies. Why are these here?" Lynn sheepishly counters, "I know I'm not supposed to eat that stuff, but I can't help it." Victor tells Lynn that he will help her be more disciplined, but only if she will make a serious effort. She agrees. Two months later, Victor finds that Lynn's eating habits have not improved. He is frustrated at her lack of self-control and views it as a major flaw in her personality.

Down-To-Earth—Pretentious

For the two months that Megan, 24, and Rudy, 24, have been dating, Rudy mostly takes her to parties and events that are trendy and often involve celebrities, including actors and musicians. Megan enjoyed the first few parties, but not the last few. When she thinks about it more, she realizes it isn't the parties that she's not thrilled with—it's Rudy himself. He seems to be caught up in his pretentious aspirations, and she doesn't like it. She decides to give up Rudy and his velvet-rope lifestyle and seek a mate who is more down-to-earth.

Energetic—Mellow

Throughout their four-year relationship, Harris, 33, and Lori, 32, have always had different energy levels. Harris can't sit still and is always looking for some physical activity to engage in. Lori, on the other hand, can be quite comfortable lying in bed and reading a novel for hours. Although such a difference might cause problems for some couples, Harris and Lori have made it work for them. They find that the key is for them to do things they enjoy together—go running, go shopping, go dancing. During the times that Harris can't sit still, he does activities on his own or with his friends. Meanwhile, Lori keeps herself occupied with more mellow activities.

Follows Rules—Is Rebellious

Justin, 23, and Ashley, 21, go to the movies on Friday night to see the latest summer action film. Concerned that the movie may sell out, Ashley buys the tickets on the internet. Even though it is three hours before the movie is to start, the movie they want to see is sold out for the time she and Justin agreed upon. Ashley then decides to buy tickets for another movie that is playing at the same time. This way, they can get into the cineplex with the other tickets, arrive early, and get seats in the movie they want to see.

On their way to the theater, Ashley explains what she did so that they could see their desired movie. Justin says, "I'm not comfortable with this. If the movie is sold out, it means that we are not supposed to see it unless we have tickets for it, which we don't." Ashley responds, "You've been talking about this movie all week, and now we have an opportunity to see it. I think we should seize this opportunity." Although still reluctant, Justin agrees, and they get seats for the movie they want to see.

The next day, when Justin thinks back to the situation, he is torn. Justin has always believed that rules are made to keep order and they should be obeyed. On the other hand, he realizes he is secretly attracted to Ashley's rebellious behavior. He plans to monitor this attribute of hers to determine if he will remain comfortable with his conflicted feelings over time, or if they will tip one way or the other.

Forgiving—Holds Grudges

Nancy, 35, and George, 36, have been together for four months. Nancy decides to analyze their relationship to determine if George is a keeper. The attribute of Forgiving—Holds Grudges jumps out as being important to her, especially since Nancy realizes that George often holds grudges—but seemingly only against her. For example, once when she agreed to pick up some soda and snacks from the supermarket on her way home and forgot to do it, George became annoyed. Nancy apologized, and George said he accepted the apology, but for the next several days he repeatedly brought up Nancy's irresponsibility.

With other people, George behaves differently. One day his brother Charles, 30, borrowed George's digital camera. A week later Charles calls George and says he accidentally dropped the camera and it's not working anymore. George was clearly annoyed with Charles, but didn't hold a grudge. Nancy didn't overhear any mention of the camera when George and Charles spoke on the phone a few days later. And when Charles and his girlfriend came over for dinner that weekend, again no mention was made of the lost camera. Nancy doesn't understand why George just holds grudges against her, but she intends to find out.

Handles Adversity Well—Handles Adversity Poorly

Theresa, 31, and Lars, 34, have been living together in a rented condo for the last two years of their three-year relationship. One day the owner of the condo tells Theresa and Lars that he has sold the apartment and they need to move out within two months. Theresa and Lars are distraught. They try to convince the owner to give them an additional two months to find a place to live. They know that finding an apartment in a good location for reasonable rent is not an easy task within a two-month timeframe.

When the owner refuses their request, they retain the services of a lawyer. The lawyer tells them there is nothing that can be done, since their lease clearly states that the owner can terminate the lease if he sells the apartment and that he only has to give them sixty days' notice. Once Lars realizes there are no options, he faces the facts and prepares for the challenge of finding a new place to live. Theresa, however, is not ready to accept the reality. She tells Lars, "It's not fair!" Lars responds, "You're right—it's not fair. However, that's what's happening, so we have no choice but to work on finding an apartment."

When Theresa continues to moan for the next two days about having to move, Lars becomes frustrated with her inability to handle adversity. He raises his voice and says, "We have to move. Deal with it." He is concerned that not only will she not help in finding an apartment, but also that her failure to deal with hard times could be a problem that may arise again at some point in the future.

High Career Ambition—Low Career Ambition

On their fifth date, Kim, 30, tells Dominic, 30, her plan to become a vice president in her company by the time she turns 35. Dominic respects her ambition, but he isn't exactly comfortable with it, because none of the women in his family ever worked outside the home. His mother and grandmothers were homemakers and raised the children. And in his last two relationships, both women were only mildly interested in their careers. He had always assumed that when he grew up he would marry a woman who would be content raising children in lieu of a career, because that is what was in his immediate world.

Although Kim does express an interest in having children, she makes it clear that she wants to continue working while raising a family. Dominic recognizes that he and Kim are not a great fit as far as career ambition goes. Although this attribute is important to him, there are many others that are more important, so he isn't overly concerned. However, he does plan on watching this attribute closely, because he wants to see if over time Kim's career ambition bothers him more or less than it does now.

High Maintenance—Low Maintenance

Julian, 29, and Sonia, 26, have been going out for two months, but may not last much longer. Before they met, Julian's friend, Dylan, 29, warned him that Sonia was "high maintenance." Julian assumed that meant Sonia wore expensive clothes and liked fancy dinners, which didn't bother him, because he likes both those things himself. Now that he's getting to know her, however, Julian finds that Sonia's high maintenance goes beyond preferring nice things. For example, while Julian understands that women typically take longer than men to get ready to go out, he believes Sonia is extreme. For a Saturday night out, it takes her a *minimum* of an hour and forty minutes to get ready. Just preparing to go to the coffee shop for breakfast takes her an hour and fifteen minutes.

Julian is also annoyed about Sonia's pickiness. When they go to the Hallmark store to buy a birthday card for her nephew, she takes a long time looking for the perfect card. "Any card will be fine," Julian states. "He's only three years old; he can't read it anyway." Julian is certain that Sonia will be unable to change her high-maintenance ways. He now has to figure out whether he can live with them.

High Sex Drive—Low Sex Drive

Diane, 24, and Keith, 25, have been dating for ten months. They both believe they have a good sex life. However, Diane wants to have sex more often than Keith does. Sometimes he turns down sex because he's unable to unwind from his stressful job. Other times it's because he'd rather watch TV. Diane decides to buy a provocative outfit from Victoria's Secret to tempt Keith and get him in the mood. She realizes the lingerie may not lead to a permanent improvement, but she wants to try pushing Keith's sexual buttons in hopes of increasing his interest.

Independent—Dependent

David, 22, and Andrea, 22, have been going out for five months. As they start spending more time together, David finds that Andrea wants to drag him everywhere—the mall, her friend's house, and, worst of all, clothes shopping. One day when she asks him to go to the grocery store with her, he responds, "Why can't you do anything by yourself?" She replies, "Don't you like going places with me?" David says, "Yes. Just not all of the time." David explains further that he sometimes likes to be by himself and have "alone time." Andrea has a difficult time understanding this, because she and her last boyfriend went everywhere together. Clearly, David and Andrea will need to resolve their very different needs on the Independent–Dependent scale before the relationship can progress.

Insecure—Secure

After dating Jasmine, 25, for three months, Malik, 30, is starting to discover that she is insecure. As they are about to leave for a dinner party, she asks, "Do I look all right? Does this dress look good on me or should I wear the blue one?" Answering sincerely, Malik says that he likes the red dress she is wearing better. As they are parking the car at the restaurant, Jasmine asks, "How does my hair look?" then adds, "I think I should have worn it up."

Malik can't help noticing other things Jasmine says and does that show her insecurity. When Jasmine bakes cookies for her niece's birthday party, she asks him to taste one. He responds "Mmmm. These are excellent, honey." She says, "Are you sure they're not too sweet?" Malik has to hold back his exasperation. He knows that Jasmine is attractive and a great cook. He just wishes that Jasmine would realize this also, and hopes he'll be able to help make her feel more secure with herself.

Intelligent—Not Intelligent

At one point in her life, Ellen, who considers herself to be very intelligent, decided to date only very smart men. Now 26, Ellen starts going out with Philip, 28, who seems to be exactly what she is looking for. She can talk to him about a variety of intellectual subjects, such as privatizing public schools and human cloning. But after six dates, Ellen finds that Philip's intelligence has limits. Although he went to an Ivy League school and seems to have an above-average IQ, Philip is not emotionally intelligent.

Ellen first noticed Philip's lack of emotional understanding when she told him how sad and concerned she was by the news that one of her friends needs an operation. Philip showed no empathy and did nothing to comfort her. It's the last straw when Ellen's cousin makes plans to visit. Ellen is thrilled about spending time with her favorite cousin, whom she hasn't seen in five years. Philip, however, seems resentful that she will be spending time with someone else, and says he doesn't see what the big deal is about spending time with her cousin. Ellen decides she is going to stop dating Philip and find someone with a more complete package of intelligence.

Jealous—Not Jealous

When Beverly, 42, stops by the office of her boyfriend Ed, 41, to drop something off for him, on the way out she notices that Ed has a new secretary, Fiona, 26, who is stunningly beautiful. After Beverly leaves, she realizes that Ed had mentioned that his old secretary had left, but he never told her that he had a new secretary. This is surprising because this is the type of thing that Ed would typically mention to her. Beverly immediately suspects that something is wrong. Perhaps Ed just forgot to tell her—but maybe he didn't mention it because he is sleeping with his secretary.

Beverly can't let it go. She calls Ed's office, and when Fiona answers his line, Beverly pretends not to know that Fiona is new, and says, "Oh, hi, Judy, it's Beverly. Is Ed in?" referring to Ed's former secretary. Fiona says, "Hi, Beverly. This is Fiona. Judy no longer works here." Beverly proceeds to ask Fiona several personal questions. That evening, when Ed comes home, he angrily asks Beverly why she was grilling his secretary. "She's a temp until I can replace Judy, and I don't appreciate your making her feel so uncomfortable."

Beverly apologizes and mulls over her own behavior. She realizes that Ed had no reason to mention a secretary who is temping, and is confident that he isn't sleeping with Fiona. However, Beverly's still not sure of the source of her jealousy. She doesn't know if it's based on her insecurity or if Ed has given her any indications that he's not being faithful. Beverly wants to figure this out, because now she realizes how potentially damaging her jealousy can be.

Kind-Hearted—Uncaring

When she was younger, Trish was always attracted to "the bad boy"—a rebellious type she found to be fascinating. Yet she never found bad boys to be boyfriend material. She never really understood why she didn't want to pursue a relationship with any of them, she just knew that it wasn't right.

Now, at 27, Trish is ready to settle down and find a mate. But first she wants to better understand the reasons why the people she dated were bad for here. What Trish finally realizes is that she is basically kind-hearted and desires a mate who is also kind-hearted. In thinking about the men in her past, she sees they were uncaring. They were all too focused on themselves and didn't seem to realize that other people—including her—have feelings. Trish is now dating Shane, 26, who is as kind-hearted as she is and very attentive to her needs. When she's cold, he offers her his jacket. Even when there is no special occasion, Shane brings her little gifts—nothing expensive, just sweet gestures that she appreciates.

Makes Me Laugh—Doesn't Make Me Laugh

Julie, 26, and Tony, 28, were briefly introduced by a mutual friend, Michelle, at a bar. The next day Julie calls Michelle inquiring about Tony. "He's great," Michelle enthuses, and gives Julie a list of Tony's positive qualities, including that he always makes her laugh. "His sense of humor is amazing!" Michelle states. Julie agrees to find out if Tony is interested in taking her out, which he is.

Julie has always valued a sense of humor, but on the date she doesn't find Tony funny at all. She concludes that he may have just been uneasy on their date. However, everything else Michelle said about him was accurate, so when he asks her out again she decides to give him another chance. Although she finds Tony to be an interesting and appealing man on the second date, his sense of humor still doesn't come through to her. Apparently she and Michelle simply have different tastes in sense of humor. Because it is so important for Julie to be with someone who can make her laugh, she's unsure if there will be a third date with Tony.

Mature—Immature

Kelly, 26, and Sean, 25, who have been on a few dates, go to the park with another couple to play tennis. Their friendly game of doubles becomes troublesome when Sean hits a shot that he thinks is "in" while the other couple calls it "out." Sean complains that they made the wrong call and he asserts that he and Kelly should get the point. When the other couple disagrees, Sean murmurs something under his breath and gets ready to play the next point. Recognizing that Sean is still upset, Kelly says, "Please let it go. It's not a big deal." Sean ignores Kelly's suggestion and proceeds to become very competitive. Every opportunity he gets, he moves close to the net so that he can emphatically hit the ball for a big winning shot. Not wanting to make a scene, Kelly doesn't say anything, but she is clearly bothered my Sean's immaturity. It's so important for her to have a mature mate that she's sure that she will not go out with Sean again.

Neat—Messy

On their first date, Jonathan, 21, picks up Sloane, 21, in his car. On the way to a club they had agreed on, Sloane notices that Jonathan's car is a mess. There is a ton of garbage on his back seat, including crumpled up papers, empty soda bottles, and a broken umbrella. On the floor in the back she sees muddy socks and a muddy soccer ball on one side, and what appears to be a moldy pile of Doritos on the other. Jonathan now has one strike against him. Sloane is not especially neat herself, but she does prefer someone who is not a total slob.

Later, when they are sitting on a couch in the club, Sloane notices that Jonathan has a hole in his pants about the size of quarter. When she points this out to him, he says, "Oh, yeah, I know about that." Strike two. Sloane doesn't like that Jonathan knowingly went out on a date wearing those pants. Later in the evening, when Jonathan spills a little of his drink on the bar, he proceeds to wipe it up with his sleeve. Strike three, Jonathan, and you are out.

Optimistic—Pessimistic

Two months ago, Samira, 31, had surgery to repair torn ligaments in her left knee. A month later, her boyfriend Omar, 30, goes with her to the doctor for a check-up. The doctor encourages Samira to stop using crutches and start walking with the use of a cane. As Samira tries her first steps without crutches, she winces in pain. "I'm never going to be as good a tennis player as I was before," she cries. "It hurts too much." The doctor informs her that her pain is normal and part of the healing process. "In fact," he says, "your knee will be even stronger than before." A week later, when Omar is at Samira's place, he asks if she has been doing the exercises that the doctor gave her. She responds, "They won't work," and changes the subject.

Later in the day, Omar thinks about how pessimistic Samira is being. At first he finds this surprising, as he has never seen Samira so down before. But after giving it additional thought, he realizes that although she's not typically a pessimist, she's never really optimistic. She's usually somewhere in the middle of the two extremes. Omar believes that, although Samira is still angry about the injury, thus bringing out her pessimistic side, this mindset of hers will go away eventually. However, he is questioning their fit for the Optimistic–Pessimistic attribute, because he has become more of an optimist over time and he is afraid she may have become more of a pessimist.

Polite—Rude

Melanie, 24, and Brandon, 23, go to the beach for their fourth date. They lie on a blanket together, reading. After a few minutes, Brandon reaches into his bag and pulls out a radio. He tunes it to an alternative-rock station and cranks up the volume. Melanie waits a minute to see if he will lower the volume, but he doesn't, so she asks him to turn it down so she can concentrate on her reading. Brandon complies, but a half hour later, when Melanie returns to their blanket after going to the refreshment stand, she finds that Brandon has once again turned up the volume on his radio. "Please turn that down!" she exclaims. "Why?" questions Brandon. "You're not reading anymore." Melanie responds, "Your music is disturbing the other people." She indicates a family to the right who is giving them unhappy looks. "So what?" Brandon responds. "No one is forcing them to stay here." Melanie is appalled at Brandon's lack of concern for other people, and decides not to go out with him again.

Private—Revealing

Nathan, 41, and Rebecca, 38, have been dating for two months, and for the first time have social plans with another couple. Halfway through the dinner conversation, Nathan is shocked when Rebecca starts telling revealing stories about herself. She discusses her bouts with anorexia and her ex-boyfriend's drug problem. Nathan believes that this information is not anyone else's business. He manages to change the topic of conversation, but he is still not pleased with Rebecca's behavior. Later that evening, he mentions to her that he is bothered by her unnecessary revelations. He points out exactly what he was uncomfortable with. Rebecca counters that she has nothing to hide and likes to be open with people. She may have to find someone else to be open with, because Nathan isn't sure if he can be with someone who wears her private life on her sleeve.

Proactive—Procrastinating

Ivan, 26, has felt as if he has been in a dead-end job for over six months. At least once a week he complains about it to his girlfriend Christine, 25, and says that he needs to find another job. Ivan's typical comment is, "Okay, I'm going to start looking next month." But the next month comes and goes and Ivan still hasn't started looking. Christine doesn't like that Ivan procrastinates so much. Realizing that he procrastinates on such an important issue, she's concerned he may procrastinate in other important situations as well.

Realistic—Unrealistic

Colin, 25, and Sandra, 25, have been dating for a year and five months. Before planning a vacation, they analyze their financial situation and realize that they don't have as much money as they'd originally planned for this trip. Unfortunately, their long-hoped-for vacation to Aruba is simply not possible on their current budget.

Colin suggests a weekend skiing trip at a lodge that's a few hours' drive away, but Sandra won't give up on the Caribbean. She tells Colin she's sure she can find a deal that will at least get them to the Bahamas. Colin tries to point out that they don't have nearly enough money, but Sandra goes ahead and spends hours trying to find cheap airline tickets and an affordable hotel. She finally gives up, having to admit that the budget simply won't stretch that far. Colin doesn't say a word, hoping that Sandra will learn to realize for herself when she is being unrealistic.

Responsible—Irresponsible

Katherine, 28, and Rick, 26, have been dating for nine months. Over the last three months, Katherine has been planning a party for her parents' 30th wedding anniversary. The week before the event, Katherine reminds Rick that the party is the following Sunday. She also asks him to make sure he will be well-rested for the party because she'll need him to help set up the room beforehand and because he'll be meeting many of her relatives for the first time. Rick agrees and looks forward to the party.

The night before the party, Rick tells Katherine that he is going out with the guys to a bar. In response Katherine says, "Please take it easy and don't drink too much tonight. I need you to be coherent tomorrow." Rick responds, "No problem. Don't worry about it." The next morning when Katherine picks up Rick, he looks like hell. When she tells him so, he replies, "I don't feel well at all," as he apparently had a hangover from the night before.

Katherine is furious at Rick's irresponsibility. She clearly communicated her desires and he agreed to them, but he didn't follow through on them. This is the first time Katherine has seen this type of behavior from Rick, and she's hoping it's the last time.

Romantic—Unromantic

Dominique, 33, often plans romantic evenings for her boyfriend Jeff, 33. Sometimes she prepares a candlelight dinner. Other times she makes them a bubble bath. Jeff appreciates Dominique's romantic gestures, but he doesn't respond in kind. Dominique is frustrated by this one-way street of romance. She tries dropping hints so that Jeff will be more romantic. One day she comments, "Marnie at my office just received a dozen roses from her boyfriend today. It was so romantic." However, Jeff doesn't pick up the hint. It's been two months and there's still been no sign of roses, tulips, or even dandelions.

Saver—Spender

Ethan, 28, and Rhonda, 27, have been going out for a year and two months. They both make roughly the same salary. But when it comes to what they each do with their income, their approaches are quite different. Ethan puts 10% of his salary into a 401K and another 10% into mutual funds. Not only does he want to make sure he has enough money for retirement, he also wants to force himself to save money for whenever he may need it. Rhonda, on the other hand, doesn't invest in a 401K or set any money aside for savings.

"I like to enjoy my money," Rhonda declares. "I can't do that by keeping it in the bank." Ethan is bothered by their stark contrast in spending styles. Looking to a possible future with Rhonda, Ethan realizes he doesn't mind spending some of his savings on her, even if he believes she has squandered hers. However, her imprudent money management bothers him.

Self-Aware—Not Self-Aware

Justine, 24, and Billy, 24, have been dating for ten months. One day after work, Billy shows up at Justine's apartment looking troubled. "What's the matter?" Justine asks. "I just got fired from my job," proclaims Billy. Justine responds, "Again!?! This is the third time in the past year that you've been fired. What are you doing wrong?" "Nothing," he says.

Justine wants to show compassion and empathize with Billy, but she can't, because she knows he is doing something wrong. They continue to talk about his problem so that Justine can identify a common link among all three situations and help Billy make any necessary adjustments to hold onto a job. After a lengthy conversation leads nowhere, Justine is bothered because Billy isn't aware of himself enough to know what caused him to be fired.

Selfish—Unselfish

Marisa, 28, has been dating Terrence, 30, for five months. He recently moved to a new apartment, and asks her to help paint his new place and go shopping for a sofa with him. Marisa agrees to do both because she likes spending time with him and she wants to help.

The requests for help do not end when the apartment is painted and the sofa is bought. Terrence continues to ask Marisa's assistance in picking things up for him, accompanying him on errands, and further decorating the apartment.

A few weeks after Terrence's apartment is completely furnished, Marisa asks Terrence to come over and help her put up her new drapes. Terrence replies that he's busy, but he can do it next week. The following week, she asks him to pick up some cat food on his way. He tells her that the store is out of the way, and he'd probably choose the wrong kind anyway.

This is the first time Marisa has experienced Terrence's selfishness and she doesn't like it at all. She doesn't know how extensive his selfishness is yet, but she will keep close tabs on it. She is particularly concerned because he is not reciprocating the helpful gestures that she has made toward him.

Sensitive—Thick-Skinned

Darren, 34, and Wendy, 31, have been dating for a year. Wendy has a major presentation at work in two days, and she asks for Darren's help in critiquing her draft of it. They sit in front of a computer for fifteen minutes while Wendy shows him ten pages of PowerPoint slides and does her verbal presentation. When she's done with the run-through, she asks him, "Well, what do you think?"

Darren thinks the presentation is only so-so and needs a few major changes, but he knows Wendy can be sensitive, so he says, "I think it's very good, but I have some ideas for improvement." Wendy responds, "Okay. Let's go through them." As Darren tells Wendy his suggestions for changes, along with the reasons for them, she becomes defensive. Darren then asks, "If you can't accept constructive criticism, then why did you ask me to critique the presentation?" Wendy apologizes and listens intently to the rest of Darren's recommended changes. But Darren knows how difficult this is for her.

Sincere—Insincere

Eve, 24, and Tomas, 25, who have been dating for eight months, are out at happy hour with a group of friends. When Eve's best friend, Rose, mentions that she just lost her job, everyone at the table offers to help in the job search, including Tomas. The next day, Tomas emails Rose a list of seven contacts. Rose doesn't hear from anyone else. She realizes that the others were merely offering general support, while Tomas was sincere and backed up his offer with specific help. When Rose calls Eve to tell her that Tomas sent her contact names and what a great guy Tomas is, Eve smiles in agreement, because Tomas's sincerity is one of the traits she likes best about him.

Smokes—Doesn't Smoke

Jack, 35, is on his third date with Donna, 33, when she takes out a cigarette. "Oh, I didn't realize you smoke," he says.

Donna responds, "I only smoke socially. If it bothers you, I don't need to smoke it." Jack then says, "I'd prefer it if you didn't." Donna says, "No problem," and puts the cigarette back into her pocketbook. The night continues without further mention of smoking.

The next day while Jack is contemplating whether he wants to go out with Donna again, he knows he has to address the smoking issue. Jack can't stand people who smoke. He thinks it is a useless and disgusting habit, and he has a hard time respecting anyone who smokes. For these reasons he's not sure if he can be with Donna. On the other hand, Donna is witty, adventurous, and has gorgeous blue eyes. And she said that she only smokes socially. So perhaps her smoking is something that he will be able to find acceptable.

Sociable—Not Sociable

Keisha, 28, and Leon, 29, have been going out for two and a half years. They both used to go out and party quite a bit. Since they are older and have both slowed down somewhat, they now have different social desires. Keisha still occasionally likes to go out drinking and dancing with their friends. Leon, however, is content to just sit at home and watch television.

When Keisha asks Leon to join her at a club one night, his response is, "Thanks anyway, but I'm going to pass. Those places are always so crowded and noisy." She replies, "Yes, and that's why I no longer like to go out four times a week. But I do like to get out and have fun sometimes." Keisha realizes their relationship will suffer if she's unable to motivate Leon to be more sociable every now and then.

Supportive—Unsupportive

Vicki, 25, who has been an avid runner her entire life, decides that she wants to run a marathon. To date, the farthest she has ever run was ten miles, and currently she is running five to six miles, three times a week. In order to be ready for the marathon, she will need to start training for it six months ahead of time. Her boyfriend Trevor, 27, says he admires her desire to run the marathon, but he becomes angry when she consistently cancels or changes plans with him in order to train. "What are you trying to prove?" he asks her. "It's not as if you're going to win any medals."

Vicki realizes that, despite his professions of support, Trevor really doesn't support her at all. She wonders if she really wants to be with someone who is so dismissive of something that has great meaning for her.

Talkative—Quiet

After going out on several dates together, Lance, 23, finds himself liking Carla, 23, more and more. One area of her personality that he deems to be a great fit is the balance their conversations have. This is in stark contrast to his last girlfriend, Sharon, 23. Lance's problem with Sharon was that she never stopped talking. It's not that Sharon wasn't interested in what Lance had to say, it's just that she loved to talk so much that she didn't give him the chance to talk much. After several discussions in which Lance asked Sharon to decrease her talking and increase her listening yielded no results, he ended their relationship. Now, with Carla, he can enjoy the normal give and take of interaction that he desires.

Trustworthy—Not Trustworthy

Bruce, 27, has always been an occasional gambler, and recently he has been placing bets at the track at least once a week. One night when he and his girlfriend, Janine, 27, are out to dinner, Bruce takes out his wallet to pay, but sees he only has two dollars left. When Janine sees that he doesn't have much cash, she is surprised. "You just took out $100 from the ATM yesterday," she says. "What happened to it?"

Bruce doesn't want to admit that he lost the money gambling, so he tells Janine that he spent it on groceries and getting his mom a birthday present. This answer is only a half-truth, since he did buy these items, but paid for them with his American Express card. Janine believes Bruce, because she doesn't have any reason not to.

Three weeks later, on a Saturday, Bruce tells Janine he is going with his friend Neil, 28, to play a highly touted golf course that day. The next day, as Bruce is driving with Janine to the mall, she finds a betting slip underneath the armrest of the passenger side of his car. The slip is dated Saturday—the day before.

Janine innocently asks, "What's this?" and shows him the slip. Busted! Bruce didn't go golfing, but instead went to the track and bet a few hundred dollars on horse racing. As he starts to play dumb, Janine figures out the truth, which Bruce eventually admits to. When Janine asks him why he tried to deceive her, he explains that he thought she would be mad that he was gambling. He was right. She is mad. But now it's not only for the gambling, it's for being untrustworthy as well.

Worldly—Naïve

Sally, 30, likes Louis, 33, on a lot of levels, but she has now found one attribute where they are a bad fit. Louis is naïve, while Sally is worldly. She always has a sense of what's going on in a wide variety of subjects, from politics and health issues to software and entertainment. Louis, a candidate for a Ph.D. in philosophy, is book smart, but knows little about these other topics. He frequently gives Sally quizzical looks when she's talking, because he's not familiar with the terms she uses. Eventually Sally realizes that she and Louis are simply not a match for this attribute, and she decides to stop seeing him.

Mapping Instructions for Section B1

Here you will continue creating your Ideal Inventory as you determine what type of person fits best with you. These instructions refer to Form 3, which starts on Page 111.

Description

All Section B exercises relate to the Spectrum Attributes. In Section B1, you will choose how important each of the Spectrum Attributes is to you. The process here is very much the same as for Section A1. The first column to the far left is labeled Attribute No. You can use this number as a reference point as you go through your Mate Map. The second column lists page numbers for easy reference to the examples in this chapter. The third column is a list of Spectrum Attributes. To the right of the Spectrum Attributes is the four-point scale of importance. This scale allows you to rate how important each Spectrum Attribute is to you.

Instructions

Read through these instructions once, then read them again as you complete Form 3, which starts on Page 111.

Starting with the first Spectrum Attribute, **Able to Relax–Uptight**, place a checkmark in the box to the right that best describes how important that Spectrum Attribute is to you. Then continue down the page until you have placed one checkmark in each row where there is a Spectrum Attribute listed. As you consider each Spectrum Attribute, you should generally decide where on the spectrum you would like your potential or current mate to be and then choose how important this attribute is to you relative to the other Spectrum Attributes. It doesn't matter exactly where on the spectrum you want your mate to be.

The purpose of identifying the level of importance for each attribute is to help you focus on the ones that are most important to you and pay less attention to the ones that are less important. To better understand each Spectrum Attribute, you may want to refer back to the examples, which begin on Page 80.

You'll notice that, below the forty-two Spectrum Attributes listed, there are spaces for four additional attributes. If you come up with any additional attributes on your own and want to map them, simply write your new Spectrum Attributes in the appropriate blank spaces on Form 3 and determine the level of importance for each. Remember, the Mate Map is a complete system that can be used as is *or* can be adjusted to suit your needs.

If, in reviewing the list of Spectrum Attributes you find a large number of attributes you consider Extremely Important, you should not mark all of them with this designation. The purpose of Mate Mapping is to prioritize what is truly most important to you. Remember that in any dating or relationship situation you will need to make compromises regarding what you are looking for and how the other person fits what you are looking for. By choosing all the attributes as Extremely Important, you would not be giving yourself the flexibility to make any compromises.

Starting on Page 111 is a blank Section B1 form for you to use (Form 3). You can also print out a copy of Form 3 from www.matemap.com by clicking on "Exercise Forms" and following the simple instructions. Alternatively, you can photocopy Form 3 from Appendix B.

Go ahead now and return to the beginning of this section, referring to the instructions as you complete Section B1.

Mapping Instructions for Section B2

The best way to understand how to complete Section B2 is to use an example. The example we will use is for the Spectrum Attribute **Responsible–Irresponsible**, which is on Page 113.

Instructions

Read through these instructions once, then read them again as you complete Form 4 on Page 115. Follow the same steps for any Spectrum Attributes that you map beyond your first one.

Step 1

Review the importance ratings of the Spectrum Attributes you mapped in Section A1 and choose the one in the Extremely Important category that is the most important to you. Write this attribute in the blank space provided. If you have difficulty determining which attribute is most important, then choose any of those rated Extremely Important. If you haven't marked any attribute as Extremely Important, than choose the attribute that is most important to you among those you deemed to be Very Important. You'll notice a heading marked **Left Pole Attribute**, which refers to the first term used to designate the Spectrum Attribute, and a heading marked **Right Pole Attribute**, which refers to the second term in the Spectrum Attribute. In the example, Samantha, a 34-year-old real estate agent, writes in "Responsible" and "Irresponsible" for the Left Pole Attribute and Right Pole Attribute respectively.

Step 2

Copy your importance rating from Section B1 into the appropriate box. In the example, Samantha places a checkmark in the box next to Extremely Important.

Step 3

Identify how you would like your mate to be, using a six-point scale. For this attribute, going from left to right, the choices are: **Most Responsible**, **Very Responsible**, **Somewhat Responsible**, **Somewhat Irresponsible**, **Very Irresponsible** and **Most Irresponsible**. In the example, Samantha places a checkmark in the box for Very Responsible.

Step 4

List the reasons that explain why you are looking for the particular trait. In the example, Samantha states, "I want someone who will follow up what he says with the appropriate action." Keep in mind that people who have used the Mate Map have found it helpful to think about experiences from past relationships (regardless of whether they are positive or negative) when rating an attribute.

Step 5

Rate your flexibility with regard in regard to this attribute, using the five-point scale. In the example, Samantha places a checkmark in the box next to Not Flexible (Dealbreaker). This means that, when she meets a man she is interested in, if he isn't Very Responsible she will probably not pursue a relationship with him.

Remember, the importance of selecting your level of flexibility is that it creates a benchmark on which to base your decisions. This way, when you meet someone you are interested in, you'll already know the attributes you are willing to compromise on, as well as those that are absolute.

Another example of Samantha's Mate Map from Section B2 can be found on Page 114. This example is for the Spectrum Attribute **Energetic–Mellow**.

On Page 115 is a blank Section B2 form for you to use (Form 4). When you have completed it, you can choose either to continue mapping other Spectrum Attributes or proceed to the next section. If you choose to map more attributes now, go to www.matemap.com, click on "Exercise Forms," and print out as many copies of Form 4 as you need. Alternatively, you can photocopy Form 4 from Appendix B. If you choose to continue to the next section, you can go back to map other Spectrum Attributes later. Remember, the more attributes you map, the better you'll understand what you are looking for and the better prepared you'll be to find the right person for you.

Go ahead now and return to the beginning of this section, referring to the instructions as you complete Section B2.

Section B1

Make a checkmark in one of the four boxes across
to identify the relative importance of each attribute to you.

Attribute No.	Page No.	Profile Attributes	Extremely Important	Very Important	Moderately Important	Slightly Important
9	80	Able to Relax—Uptight				
10	81	Adaptable—Unadaptable				
11	81	Affectionate—Not Affectionate				
12	82	Assertive—Unassertive				
13	82	Calm—Hotheaded				
14	83	Compromises—Doesn't Compromise				
15	84	Decisive—Indecisive				
16	85	Disciplined—Has No Self-Control				
17	85	Down-To-Earth—Pretentious				
18	86	Energetic—Mellow				
19	86	Follows Rules—Is Rebellious				
20	87	Forgiving—Holds Grudges				
21	88	Handles Adversity Well—Handles Adversity Poorly				
22	89	High Career Ambition—Low Career Ambition				
23	89	High Maintenance—Low Maintenance				
24	90	High Sex Drive—Low Sex Drive				
25	90	Independent—Dependent				
26	91	Insecure—Secure				
27	92	Intelligent—Not Intelligent				
28	92	Jealous—Not Jealous				
29	93	Kind-hearted—Uncaring				
30	94	Makes Me Laugh—Doesn't Make Me Laugh				
31	94	Mature—Immature				

Section B1

Make a checkmark in one of the four boxes across
to identify the relative importance of each attribute to you.

Attribute No.	Page No.	Profile Attributes	Extremely Important	Very Important	Moderately Important	Slightly Important
32	95	Neat—Messy				
33	96	Optimistic—Pessimistic				
34	96	Polite—Rude				
35	97	Private—Revealing				
36	98	Proactive—Procrastinating				
37	98	Realistic—Unrealistic				
38	98	Responsible—Irresponsible				
39	99	Romantic—Unromantic				
40	100	Saver—Spender				
41	100	Self-Aware—Not Self-Aware				
42	101	Selfish—Unselfish				
43	101	Sensitive—Thick-Skinned				
44	102	Sincere—Insincere				
45	102	Smokes—Doesn't Smoke				
46	103	Sociable—Not Sociable				
47	104	Supportive—Unsupportive				
48	104	Talkative—Quiet				
49	105	Trustworthy—Not Trustworthy				
50	106	Worldly—Naïve				
(Add one)						
(Add one)						
(Add one)						
(Add one)						

Section B2

Example 1

Step 1	Write in an attribute you determined to be of high importance in Section B1.	Spectrum Attribute 1

Spectrum Attribute 1

Left Pole Attribute

Right Pole Attribute

Responsible

Irresponsible

Step 2

How important is this attribute to you?

Extremely Important	✓
Very Important	
Moderately Important	
Slightly Important	

Step 3

Ideally, what are you looking for (and not looking for)?

Most	Very	Somewhat	Somewhat	Very	Most
	✓				

Step 4

What are the reasons for your preference?

I want someone who will follow up what he says with the appropriate action.

Step 5

How flexible are you about your ideal?

Not Flexible (Dealbreaker)	✓
Slightly Flexible	
Moderately Flexible	
Very Flexible	
Extremely Flexible	

Section B2

Example 2

Step 1

Write in an attribute you determined to be of high importance in Section B1.

Spectrum Attribute 2

Left Pole Attribute	Right Pole Attribute
Energetic	Mellow

Step 2

How important is this attribute to you?

Extremely Important	✓
Very Important	
Moderately Important	
Slightly Important	

Step 3

Ideally, what are you looking for (and not looking for)?

Most	Very	Somewhat	Somewhat	Very	Most
			✓		

Step 4

What are the reasons for your preference?

I'm always on the go and I prefer someone who is more mellow than I am because I need someone who can "mellow me out."

Step 5

How flexible are you about your ideal?

Not Flexible (Dealbreaker)	
Slightly Flexible	
Moderately Flexible	✓
Very Flexible	
Extremely Flexible	

Section B2

Form 4

Step 1

Write in an attribute you determined to be of high importance in Section B1.

Spectrum Attribute 1

Left Pole Attribute   Right Pole Attribute

_____   _____

Step 2

How important is this attribute to you?

Extremely Important	
Very Important	
Moderately Important	
Slightly Important	

Step 3

Ideally, what are you looking for (and not looking for)?

Most	Very	Somewhat	Somewhat	Very	Most

Step 4

What are the reasons for your preference?

Step 5

How flexible are you about your ideal?

Not Flexible (Dealbreaker)	
Slightly Flexible	
Moderately Flexible	
Very Flexible	
Extremely Flexible	

CHAPTER

9

The Physical Attributes

Here you will determine your preferred physical type to complete the third and final section of your Ideal Inventory.

Mapping Instructions for Section C1

These instructions refer to Form 5 on Page 121.

Description

All Section C exercises relate to the Physical Attributes. In Section C1, you will choose how important each of the Physical Attributes is to you, much the same way you did in Sections A1 and B1. The first four columns are the same, but there is now a fifth column as well. The first column to the far left is labeled Attribute No. You can use this number as a reference point as you go through your Mate Map. The second column lists page numbers for easy reference to the examples in this chapter. The third column is a list of Physical Attributes. To the right of the Physical Attributes is the four-point scale of importance. This scale allows you to rate how important each Physical Attribute is to you. The fifth column shows examples of what you might specifically be looking for or looking to avoid regarding each of the Physical Attributes.

Instructions

Read through these instructions once, then read them again as you complete Form 5 on Page 121.

Starting with the first Physical Attribute, **Hair**, place a checkmark in the box to the right that best describes how important that Physical Attribute is to you. Then continue down the page until you have placed one checkmark in each row where there is a Physical Attribute listed. As you consider each Physical Attribute, you should also be thinking about how important this attribute is to you relative to the other Physical Attributes.

The purpose of identifying the level of importance for each attribute is to help you focus on the ones most important to you and pay less attention to the ones that are less important.

You'll notice that, below the sixteen Physical Attributes listed, there are spaces for two additional attributes. If you come up with any additional attributes on your own and want to map them, simply write your new Physical Attributes in the appropriate blank spaces on Form 5 and determine the level of importance for each. Remember, the Mate Map is a complete system that can be used as is *or* can be adjusted to suit your needs.

If, in reviewing the list of Physical Attributes, you find a large number of attributes you consider Extremely Important, you should not mark all of them with this designation. The purpose of Mate Mapping is to prioritize what is truly most important to you. Remember that in any dating or relationship situation you will need to make compromises regarding what you are looking for and how the other person fits what you are looking for. By choosing all the attributes as Extremely Important, you would not be giving yourself the flexibility to make any compromises.

On Page 121 is a blank Section C1 form for you to use (Form 5). You can also print out a copy of Form 5 from www.matemap.com by clicking on "Exercise Forms" and following the simple instructions. Alternatively, you can photocopy Form 5 from Appendix B.

Go ahead now and return to the beginning of this section, referring to the instructions as you complete Section C1.

Mapping Instructions for Section C2

The best way to understand how to complete Section C2 is to use an example. The example we will use is for the Physical Attribute **Hair**, which is on Page 122.

Instructions

Read through these instructions once, then read them again as you complete Form 6 on Page 124. Follow the same steps for any Physical Attributes that you map beyond your first one.

Step 1

Review the importance ratings of the Physical Attributes you mapped in Section C1 and choose the one in the Extremely Important category that is the most important to you. Write this attribute in the blank space provided. If you have difficulty determining which attribute is most important, then choose any of those rated Extremely Important. If you haven't marked any attribute as Extremely Important, then choose the attribute that is most important to you among those you deemed to be Very Important. In the example, Ron, a 27-year-old civil engineer, chooses Hair and writes "Hair" on the blank line.

Step 2

Copy your importance rating from Section C1 into the appropriate box. In the example, Ron places a checkmark in the box next to Extremely Important.

Step 3

With regard to this attribute, write in what you are looking for and not looking for in a mate. Be as specific as possible. In the example, Ron writes, "I prefer long hair that is at least touching the shoulders and up to a few inches longer than that. I prefer dark hair, but all colors are fine. I have no preference for straight or curly hair."

Step 4

List the reasons that explain why you are looking for the particular trait. In the example, Ron writes: "I find long hair to be part of a woman's femininity, which is extremely important to me. I also like the way it feels when I run my fingers through a woman's long hair." Again, it is often helpful, if appropriate, to refer to good or bad circumstances from a past relationship.

Step 5

Rate your flexibility with regard to this attribute, using the five-point scale. In the example, Ron places a checkmark in the box next to Slightly Flexible. This means that when he meets a woman he is interested in, if her hair is very short and she plans on keeping it short, he may not pursue her. However, of course he is unable to make an absolute determination until he can apply his Slight Flexibility to an actual dating situation.

Another example of Ron's Mate Map from Section C2 can be found on Page 123. This example is for the Physical Attribute **Height**.

On Page 124 is a blank Section C2 form for you to use (Form 6). When you have completed it, you can choose either to continue mapping other Physical Attributes or proceed directly to the next section. If you choose to map more attributes now, go to www.matemap.com, click on "Exercise Forms," and print out as many copies of Form 6 as you need. Alternatively, you can photocopy Form 6 from Appendix B. If you choose to proceed to the next section, you can go back to map other Physical Attributes later. Remember, the more attributes you map, the better you'll understand what you are looking for and the better prepared you'll be to make the best relationship decisions for yourself.

Go ahead now and return to the beginning of this section, referring to the instructions as you complete Section C2.

Section C1
Form 5

Make a checkmark in one of the four boxes across
to identify the relative importance of each attribute to you.

Attribute No.	Physical Attributes	Extremely Important	Very Important	Moderately Important	Slightly Important	Examples
51	Hair					short, blonde, straight, balding
52	Eyes					brown, blue, big, oval-shaped
53	Face					round, square jaw, high cheekbones
54	Smile					eyes light up, shows teeth
55	Lips					full, thin
56	Teeth					straight, pearly white, has full set
57	Nose					big, small, narrow, flaring nostrils
58	Ears					big, small, stick out
59	Skin					olive, smooth, pasty white
60	Height					5'1", 5'8", 6'4"
61	Body					average frame, heavy, muscular
62	Sex Appeal					very sexy, not so sexy
63	Cuteness					very cute, not so cute
64	Pretty/Handsome					not pretty, quite handsome
65	Feminine/Masculine					very feminine, exudes masculinity
66	Overall Look					dresses well, natural, has tattoos
(Add one)						
(Add one)						

Section C2

Example 1

Step 1	Write in an attribute you determined to be of high importance in Section C1.	Physical Attribute 1
		Hair

Step 2 — How important is this attribute to you?

Extremely Important	✓
Very Important	
Moderately Important	
Slightly Important	

Step 3 — Ideally, what are you looking for (and not looking for)?

I prefer long hair that is at least touching the shoulders and up to a few inches longer than that. I prefer dark hair, but all colors are fine. I have no preference for straight or curly hair.

Step 4 — What are the reasons for your preference?

I find long hair to be part of a woman's femininity, which is extremely important to me. I also like the way it feels when I run my fingers through a woman's long hair.

Step 5 — How flexible are you about your ideal?

Not Flexible (Dealbreaker)	
Slightly Flexible	✓
Moderately Flexible	
Very Flexible	
Extremely Flexible	

Section C2

Example 2

Step 1

Write in an attribute you determined to be of high importance in Section C1.

Physical Attribute 2

Height

Step 2

How important is this attribute to you?

Extremely Important	✓
Very Important	
Moderately Important	
Slightly Important	

Step 3

Ideally, what are you looking for (and not looking for)?

I would like my mate to be between 5'0" and 5'6".

Step 4

What are the reasons for your preference?

I find that I'm just not attracted to tall women.

Step 5

How flexible are you about your ideal?

Not Flexible (Dealbreaker)	
Slightly Flexible	
Moderately Flexible	✓
Very Flexible	
Extremely Flexible	

Section C2
Form 6

Step 1

Write in an attribute you determined to be of high importance in Section C1.

Physical Attribute 1

_____

Step 2

How important is this attribute to you?

Extremely Important	
Very Important	
Moderately Important	
Slightly Important	

Step 3

Ideally, what are you looking for (and not looking for)?

Step 4

What are the reasons for your preference?

Step 5

How flexible are you about your ideal?

Not Flexible (Dealbreaker)	
Slightly Flexible	
Moderately Flexible	
Very Flexible	
Extremely Flexible	

THREE

The Mate Map:
Phases II, III, IV and V

10

Phase II— Mapping Your Mate

In Phase I, you started to build your Mate Map by completing the exercises in Sections A, B and C, which resulted in the creation of your Ideal Inventory. Now, in Phase II, you will build on your Mate Map further by applying your Ideal Inventory to a specific person. This person can be someone you have been on one or more dates with or someone with whom you are currently in a relationship. Regardless of whether this person is a potential mate or your current mate, I'll refer to this person as "your mate" for the remainder of the book.

If you are single and not currently dating, you will not yet be able to complete the exercises in the remaining phases of the Mate Map. Still, go through the process to learn the next steps so you'll discover even more about the Relationship Essentials and be prepared for when you meet someone you're interested in.

In Phase II, you will apply the Profile, Spectrum and Physical Attributes you mapped in Phase I. Here you will also map Chemistry, as well as Love, as long as it's applicable.

There are several sets of exercises in this chapter, so a quick glance ahead at these may seem daunting. However, don't be deterred, as they are more simple when you do them than they look at first. Each exercise has easy-to-follow instructions to lead you through. Before you know it, you'll be able to map the Phase II exercises without the instructions. They really are that simple.

There are several exercises here, so you will have to put your mind to work. While there is extra effort involved, you'll find it pays dividends. One of the participants in the Mate Map Study said it best: "The Mate Map requires work, but so does any good relationship."

Keep It Private for Now

The Mate Map was designed to be used individually, even if you're in a relationship. The reason is that the assessment of a potential or current mate is a personal matter and shouldn't necessarily be shared with the person you map. For example, if you mark on your Mate Map that your new boyfriend rates poorly for the Physical Attribute **Sex Appeal**, it is probably not in your best interest for him to know about this. As you'll see in Chapter 12 and Chapter 14, there are appropriate times for you to let your potential or current mate know about certain Mate Map discoveries. However, until those times arise, I advise you to not share your personal Mate Map with your mate. After you learn more about the Mate Map and want a potential or current mate to learn it as well, go ahead and introduce it to him or her, but continue to keep your Mate Maps separate until you are shown what to discuss and when.

Mapping Instructions for Section A3

These instructions refer to the example on Page 131. This example is a continuation of the one for the Profile Attribute **Age** from Section A2 (Page 73).

Description

In Section A3, you will choose how well your mate matches what you are looking for regarding the Profile Attributes.

Instructions

Read through these instructions once, then read them again as you complete Form 7 on Page 133. Follow the same steps for any Profile Attributes that you map beyond your first one.

Step 1

Copy in the Profile Attribute you chose in Section A2. Continuing with the example from Section A2, Debbie, the 29-year-old graphic designer, copies in "Age."

Step 2

Describe your mate in terms of the chosen attribute. In the example, Debbie, describing Jason, the guy she is seeing, states: "He is 27 years old."

Step 3

Describe how well your mate fits with you for this attribute. In the example, Debbie writes: "I'm uncomfortable with him being two years younger than me, as my past boyfriends were all at least three years older than me."

Step 4

Rate your Personality Fit with your mate for this attribute by making a checkmark next to the appropriate rating on the six-point scale: **Excellent**, **Very Good**, **Good**, **Fair**, **Poor** and **None** (No Fit). This rating is a measure of how closely your mate fits with what you're looking for. In the example, Debbie places a checkmark in the box next to Fair, since the age difference bothers her.

Another example of Section A3 can be found on Page 132. This example is for the Profile Attribute **Education Level**, and is a continuation of the example for this attribute from Section A2 (Page 74).

On Page 133 is a blank Section A3 form for you to use (Form 7). When you have completed it, you can choose either to continue mapping other Profile Attributes or proceed to the next section. If you choose to map more attributes now, go to www.matemap.com, click on "Exercise Forms," and print out as many copies of Form 7 as you need. Alternatively, you can photocopy Form 7 from Appendix B. If you choose to

Section A3

Example 1

Step 1

Copy in the Profile Attribute you chose in Section A2.	Profile Attribute 1 Age

Step 2

Describe your mate.	He is 27 years old.

Step 3

Describe your Personality Fit.	I'm uncomfortable with him being two years younger than me, as my past boyfriends were all at least three years older than me.

Step 4

Rate your Personality Fit with your mate by making a checkmark next to the appropriate category to the right.

Excellent	
Very Good	
Good	
Fair	✓
Poor	
None	

Section A3

Example 2

Step 1

Copy in the Profile Attribute you chose in Section A2.	Profile Attribute 2
	Education Level

Step 2

Describe your mate.	He has a college degree.

Step 3

Describe your Personality Fit.	He has what I'm looking for.

Step 4

Rate your Personality Fit with your mate by making a checkmark next to the appropriate category to the right.

Excellent	✓
Very Good	
Good	
Fair	
Poor	
None	

Section A3

Form 7

Step 1

Copy in the Profile Attribute you chose in Section A2.

Profile Attribute 1

_____

Step 2

Describe your mate.

Step 3

Describe your Personality Fit.

Step 4

Rate your Personality Fit with your mate by making a checkmark next to the appropriate category to the right.

Excellent	
Very Good	
Good	
Fair	
Poor	
None	

133

continue to the next section, you can go back to map other Profile Attributes later. Remember, the more attributes you map, the better you'll understand what you are looking for and the better prepared you'll be to make the best relationship decisions for yourself.

Go ahead now and return to the beginning of this section, referring to the instructions as you complete Section A3.

Mapping Instructions for Section B3

These instructions refer to the example on Page 136. This example is a continuation of the one for the Spectrum Attribute **Responsible–Irresponsible** from Section B2 (Page 113).

Description

In Section B3, you will choose how well your mate matches what you are looking for regarding the Spectrum Attributes.

Instructions

Read through these instructions once, then read them again as you complete Form 8 on Page 138. Follow the same steps for any Spectrum Attributes that you map beyond your first one.

Step 1

Copy in the Spectrum Attribute you chose in Section B2. Continuing with the example from Section B2, Samantha, the 34-year-old real estate agent, copies in "Responsible" and "Irresponsible."

Step 2

Identify your mate's position on this spectrum using a six-point scale. For this attribute, going from left to right, the choices are: Most Responsible, Very Responsible, Somewhat Responsible, Somewhat Irresponsible, Very Irresponsible and Most Irresponsible. In the example, Samantha places a checkmark in the box for Very Irresponsible, to describe her boyfriend Zach, 34.

Step 3

Describe how well your mate fits with you for this attribute. In the example, Samantha writes: "Last week he showed up a half hour late for my important business dinner and was underdressed. This week he said he would take care of making plans for my birthday and never did."

Step 4

Rate your Personality Fit with your mate for this attribute by making a checkmark next to the appropriate rating on the six-point scale: Excellent, Very Good, Good, Fair, Poor and None. In the example, Samantha places a checkmark in the box next to Poor, since she doesn't want to be with someone who is Very Irresponsible.

Another example of Section B3 can be found on Page 137. This example is for the Spectrum Attribute **Energetic–Mellow**, and is a continuation of the example for this attribute from Section B2 (Page 114).

On Page 138 is a blank Section B3 form for you to use (Form 8). When you have completed it, you can choose either to continue mapping other Spectrum Attributes or proceed to

Section B3

Example I

Step I

Copy in the Spectrum
Attribute you chose
in Section B2.

Spectrum Attribute I

Left Pole Attribute	Right Pole Attribute
Responsible	Irresponsible

Step 2

Describe your mate.

Most	Very	Somewhat	Somewhat	Very	Most
				✓	

Step 3

Describe your
Personality Fit.

He is irresponsible in many ways. Last week he showed up a half hour late for my important business dinner and was underdressed. This week he said he would take care of making plans for my birthday and never did.

Step 4

Rate your Personality Fit
with your mate by making
a checkmark next to
the appropriate category
to the right.

Excellent	
Very Good	
Good	
Fair	
Poor	✓
None	

Section B3

Example 2

Step 1		Spectrum Attribute 2	

Step 1

Copy in the Spectrum Attribute you chose in Section B2.

Spectrum Attribute 2

Left Pole Attribute

Right Pole Attribute

Energetic

Mellow

Step 2

Describe your mate.

Most	Very	Somewhat	Somewhat	Very	Most
					✓

Step 3

Describe your Personality Fit.

Although I prefer someone who is more mellow than I am, he may be too mellow for me.

Step 4

Rate your Personality Fit with your mate by making a checkmark next to the appropriate category to the right.

Excellent	
Very Good	
Good	
Fair	✓
Poor	
None	

Section B3

Form 8

Step 1

Copy in the Spectrum Attribute you chose in Section B2.

Spectrum Attribute 1

Left Pole Attribute

Right Pole Attribute

_____   _____

Step 2

Describe your mate.

Most	Very	Somewhat	Somewhat	Very	Most

Step 3

Describe your Personality Fit.

Step 4

Rate your Personality Fit with your mate by making a checkmark next to the appropriate category to the right.

Excellent	
Very Good	
Good	
Fair	
Poor	
None	

the next section. If you choose to map more attributes now, go to www.matemap.com, click on "Exercise Forms," and print out as many copies of Form 8 as you need. Alternatively, you can photocopy Form 8 from Appendix B. If you choose to continue to the next section, you can go back to map other Spectrum Attributes later. Remember, the more attributes you map, the better you'll understand what you are looking for and the better prepared you'll be to find the right person for you.

Go ahead now and return to the beginning of this section, referring to the instructions as you complete Section B3.

Mapping Instructions for Section C3

These instructions refer to the example on Page 141. This example is a continuation of the one for the Physical Attribute **Hair** from Section C2 (Page 122).

Description

In Section C3, you will choose how well your mate matches what you are looking for regarding the Physical Attributes.

Instructions

Read through these instructions once, then read them again as you complete Form 9 on Page 143. Follow the same steps for any Physical Attributes that you map beyond your first one.

Step 1

Copy in the Physical Attribute you chose in Section C2. Continuing with the example from Section C2, Ron, the 27-year-old civil engineer, copies in "Hair."

Step 2

Describe your mate in terms of the chosen attribute. In the example Ron, writes, "Her hair is long, below the shoulders, dark brown, and straight, " referring to Shelly, 26, who he has recently started dating.

Step 3

Describe how well your mate fits with you for this attribute. In the example, Ron writes: "It's an excellent fit. She also changes her look sometimes (wears a headband, makes it curly), which I like."

Step 4

Rate your Personality Fit with your mate for this attribute by making a checkmark next to the appropriate rating on the six-point scale: Excellent, Very Good, Good, Fair, Poor and None. In the example, Ron places a checkmark in the box next to Excellent, since his mate has exactly what he is looking for.

Another example of Section C3 can be found on Page 142. This example is for the Physical Attribute **Height**, and is a continuation of the example for this attribute from Section C2 (Page 123).

On Page 143 is a blank Section C3 form for you to use (Form 9). When you have completed it, you can choose either to continue mapping other Physical Attributes or proceed directly to the next section. If you choose to map more attributes now, go to www.matemap.com, click on "Exercise Forms," and print out as many copies of Form 9 as you need. Alternatively, you can photocopy Form 9 from Appendix B. If you choose to proceed to the next section, you can go back to map

Section C3

Example 1

Step 1

Copy in the Physical Attribute you chose in Section C2.	Physical Attribute 1
	Hair

Step 2

Describe your mate.	Her hair is long, below the shoulders, dark brown, and straight.

Step 3

Describe your Physical Attraction Fit.	It's an excellent fit. She also changes her look sometimes (wears a headband, makes it curly), which I like.

Step 4

Rate your Physical Attraction Fit with your mate by making a checkmark next to the appropriate category to the right.	Excellent	✓
	Very Good	
	Good	
	Fair	
	Poor	
	None	

141

Section C3

Example 2

Step 1

Copy in the Physical
Attribute you chose
in Section C2.

Physical Attribute 2

Height

Step 2

Describe your mate.

She is 5'9".

Step 3

Describe your
Physical Attraction Fit.

She is taller than I would like. I'm 5'10" and when
she wears heels she is taller than me, which makes
me uncomfortable.

Step 4

Rate your Physical Attraction
Fit with your mate by
making a checkmark
next to the appropriate
category to the right.

Excellent	
Very Good	
Good	
Fair	✓
Poor	
None	

Step 1

Copy in the Physical
Attribute you chose
in Section C2.

Physical Attribute 1

_____

Step 2

Describe your mate.

Step 3

Describe your
Physical Attraction Fit.

Step 4

Rate your Physical Attraction
Fit with your mate by
making a checkmark
next to the appropriate
category to the right.

Excellent	
Very Good	
Good	
Fair	
Poor	
None	

other Physical Attributes later. Remember, the more attributes you map, the better you'll understand what you are looking for and the better prepared you'll be to make the best relationship decisions for yourself.

Go ahead now and return to the beginning of this section, referring to the instructions as you complete Section C3.

Mapping Chemistry

As mentioned in Chapter 4, mapping Chemistry is different from mapping the Profile, Spectrum and Physical Attributes because Chemistry cannot be mapped with any level of certainty until there is another person in the picture. Here, you'll be able to determine how well you fit with your mate in terms of Chemistry.

Before you complete Section D (Chemistry) of your Mate Map, you should first understand a truth about mapping Chemistry.

MAPPING CHEMISTRY TRUTH I
Chemistry doesn't change dramatically over the course of a relationship.

The Chemistry between any two people is natural and instinctive and somewhat beyond our control. If you have bad Chemistry with someone, there is usually nothing you can do to achieve great Chemistry. And, if you have excellent Chemistry, it is unlikely that this Chemistry will decrease dramatically. There are exceptions to this second example, such as infidelity, which can permanently spoil the Chemistry between two partners. But, if there are problems in an ongoing relationship, they are probably due to a decrease in Personality Fit, Physical Attraction and/or Love, rather than a decrease in Chemistry.

Although large changes in Chemistry are unlikely, incremental changes—either positive or negative—can take place at various times. Chemistry decreases mostly because of external factors. For example, having prolonged stress or spending a lot of time apart can cause a decrease in Chemistry. Not surprisingly, increases in Chemistry are also caused by external factors, such as moving in together or having a job change that leaves the couple more time to spend together.

Mapping Instructions for Section D

These instructions refer to the example on Page 147.

Description

In Section D, you will determine how compatible you are with your mate in terms of Chemistry.

Instructions

Read through these instructions once, then read them again as you complete Form 10 on Page 153.

As you recall from Chapter 4, there are six different Chemistry Categories: (Category 1) **Verbal Communication**, (Category 2) **Nonverbal Communication**, (Category 3) **Sexual Compatibility**, (Category 4) **Desire To Be Together**, (Category 5) **Ease of Getting Along**, and (Category 6) **Influence**. We're going to look at an example of Section D using Category 1, Verbal Communication, which is on Page 147.

For each category, think of up to three anecdotes that specifically describe the Chemistry between you and your mate. Here, for the first anecdote of Chemistry Category 1, Verbal Communication, Joe, a 23-year-old musician, writes in: "Our conversations flow with incredible ease," when referring to his girlfriend, Carrie, 23. He rates this anecdote as Excellent by placing a checkmark in the appropriate box. For the second anecdote, he writes in: "For some reason, when it comes to talking about our relationship, I don't open up as much as I should." Recognizing he would like to open up more to Carrie in relationship discussions, Joe rates this anecdote as Fair. For the third anecdote, Joe states: "Although I thoroughly explain any favor I ask of her in detail, she completely misunderstands me." He rates this anecdote of Verbal Communication as Poor.

Starting on Page 148 there are examples of anecdotes from the other five Chemistry Categories that Joe mapped, which will help you better understand how to map Chemistry.

On Page 153 is a blank Section D form for you to use (Form 10). When mapping a Chemistry Category for the first time, you can choose any of the six categories you'd like. After you have mapped one category, you can choose either to continue mapping other Chemistry Categories or proceed directly to the next section. If you choose to map more categories now, go to www.matemap.com, click on "Exercise Forms," and print out as many copies of Form 10 as you need. Alternatively, you can photocopy Form 10 from Appendix B. If you choose to proceed to the next section, you can go back to map other Chemistry Categories later. The more categories you map, the better you'll understand what you are looking for and the better prepared you'll be to make the best relationship decisions for yourself.

Section D
Example 1

Chemistry Category 1
Verbal Communication
Measure the clarity of your verbal interactions.

Provide three anecdotes and rate each one.

Anecdote 1		
Our conversations flow with incredible ease.	Excellent	✓
	Very Good	
	Good	
	Fair	
	Poor	
	None	

Anecdote 2		
For some reason, when it comes to talking about our relationship, I don't open up as much as I should.	Excellent	
	Very Good	
	Good	
	Fair	✓
	Poor	
	None	

Anecdote 3		
Although I thoroughly explain any favor I ask of her in detail, she completely misunderstands me.	Excellent	
	Very Good	
	Good	
	Fair	
	Poor	
	None	✓

Section D

Example 2

| Chemistry Category 2 |
| Nonverbal Communication |
| Measure how you connect nonverbally. |

Provide three anecdotes and rate each one.

Anecdote 1		
In a group conversation I shot her a look to change the subject and she toned down what she was saying, but kept the same conversation going.		

Excellent	
Very Good	
Good	
Fair	✓
Poor	
None	

Anecdote 2		
When we are at a party and on opposite sides of the room, I can feel her eyes on me while I'm talking to friends and my back is turned to her.		

Excellent	✓
Very Good	
Good	
Fair	
Poor	
None	

Anecdote 3		
If I'm feeling down, she can make me feel better by a simple touch.		

Excellent	
Very Good	✓
Good	
Fair	
Poor	
None	

Section D

Example 3

Chemistry Category 3	
Sexual Chemistry	
Measure how well you fit sexually.	

Provide three anecdotes and rate each one.

Anecdote 1		
	Excellent	✓
	Very Good	
	Good	
I don't ever want to stop kissing her because it makes me feel great.	Fair	
	Poor	
	None	

Anecdote 2		
	Excellent	
	Very Good	✓
She is usually able to interpret my sounds and movements. But when she doesn't, I feel comfortable directing her in what I would like her to do.	Good	
	Fair	
	Poor	
	None	

Anecdote 3		
	Excellent	✓
	Very Good	
	Good	
Even when I'm busy and not "in the mood," she still turns me on.	Fair	
	Poor	
	None	

Section D

Example 4

Provide three anecdotes and rate each one.

Anecdote 1		
We always have such a great time together. It's not the same when I have plans without her.	Excellent	✓
	Very Good	
	Good	
	Fair	
	Poor	
	None	

Anecdote 2		
Even the thought of seeing her later today puts a smile on my face.	Excellent	
	Very Good	✓
	Good	
	Fair	
	Poor	
	None	

Anecdote 3		
When I went out of town for a few days, I didn't miss her as much as I thought I would.	Excellent	
	Very Good	
	Good	
	Fair	✓
	Poor	
	None	

Section D

Example 5

<table>
<tr><td colspan="2" style="text-align:center">Chemistry Category 5
Ease Of Getting Along
Measure how comfortable you are with him or her.</td></tr>
</table>

Provide three anecdotes and rate each one.

Anecdote 1		
	Excellent	✓
	Very Good	
I feel that we've known each other for years, although we've only been together for a few months.	Good	
	Fair	
	Poor	
	None	

Anecdote 2		
	Excellent	
	Very Good	✓
When we're together, I'm comfortable with long periods of silence.	Good	
	Fair	
	Poor	
	None	

Anecdote 3		
	Excellent	✓
	Very Good	
She rarely gets on my nerves.	Good	
	Fair	
	Poor	
	None	

Section D

Example 6

Chemistry Category 6
Influence
Measure how well he or she naturally improves you.

Provide three anecdotes and rate each one.

Anecdote 1		
Just by being with her, I find myself having more confidence and being more assertive.	Excellent	
	Very Good	✓
	Good	
	Fair	
	Poor	
	None	

Anecdote 2		
She is such a good person that it has naturally made me more kind-hearted.	Excellent	✓
	Very Good	
	Good	
	Fair	
	Poor	
	None	

Anecdote 3		
I have matured somewhat since I started dating her.	Excellent	
	Very Good	
	Good	✓
	Fair	
	Poor	
	None	

Section D
Form 10

Chemistry Category

Provide three anecdotes and rate each one.

Anecdote 1		

	Excellent	
	Very Good	
	Good	
	Fair	
	Poor	
	None	

Anecdote 2		

	Excellent	
	Very Good	
	Good	
	Fair	
	Poor	
	None	

Anecdote 3		

	Excellent	
	Very Good	
	Good	
	Fair	
	Poor	
	None	

Go ahead now and return to the beginning of this section, referring to the instructions as you complete Section D.

Mapping Love

Note that Love is often not applicable during the early stages of a relationship. If you are in a relationship where it's too early to assess Love, then you should not yet complete Section E (Love). However, even if Love does not apply yet, I urge you to read through this section, and the category anecdotes in particular, so that you will be prepared when you do fall in Love.

Before you complete Section E of your Mate Map, you should first understand a truth about mapping Love.

MAPPING LOVE TRUTH I
Check your Love filter.

In order to assess the level of Love in a relationship, we must first have a good idea of what Love is, based on our own beliefs about Love. I refer to these beliefs as our "Love filter," which is the area where we store our general beliefs about Love. Our Love filter is constructed over our lifetime. It starts with our childhood observations of the adult relationships around us, such as those of our parents and grandparents. Starting with our teen years and continuing throughout adulthood, we create more beliefs as we experience our own relationships. We further add to our Love filter as we continue to observe other relationships around us.

The hope is that each of us has a strong Love filter, which is marked by having a true sense of what Love is all about.

However, many people may have a warped Love filter. This can happen because their parents had an unhealthy relationship when they were growing up, because one or both of their parents did not raise them, or because they have been in unhealthy relationships themselves. If you find you don't have a solid grasp of what Love is, I recommend consulting with a therapist.

Note that when completing Section E, you may find yourself comparing your level of Love in a past relationship to a current relationship, which is quite understandable. The problem with this direct comparison is that it leads you to ask the question "Is the level of Love in my current relationship better than that of my last one?" Unfortunately, such a direct comparison does not allow you to fully answer the more important question: "Does this relationship meet my expectations of what Love should be?" Rather than directly comparing the levels of Love from one relationship to another, it's better to assess the Love from each previous relationship as it applies to your Love filter. The comparison to your Love filter will indicate whether or not each relationship meets your general expectations of a loving relationship. Then apply your updated understanding of Love when mapping your mate.

Mapping Instructions for Section E

These instructions refer to the example on Page 158.

Description

In Section E, you will determine how compatible you are with your mate in terms of Love. You may have noticed that, just as with Chemistry, you have not completed any section for Love yet. Since Love takes place with the interaction between two people, it cannot be properly assessed until there is a significant other with whom you can measure Love.

Instructions

Read through these instructions once, then read them again as you complete Form 11 on Page 164.

As you recall from Chapter 5, there are six different Love Categories: (Category 1) **What You Feel**, (Category 2) **Importance**, (Category 3) **What You Find Special (Or Not Special)**, (Category 4) **Love Fulfillment**, (Category 5) **Love Compatibility**, (Category 6) **Changes My Outlook For The Better (Or Worse)**. We're going to look at an example of Section E using Love Category 1, What You Feel, which is on Page 158.

For each category, think of up to three anecdotes that specifically describe the Love between you and your mate. Here, for the first anecdote of Love Category 1, What You Feel, Eileen, a 26-year-old accountant who is mapping her boyfriend Seth, 30, writes in: "Whenever I'm with him I feel safe and secure." She rates this anecdote as Excellent by placing a checkmark in the appropriate box. For the second anecdote, Eileen writes in: "He doesn't actively look out for my well-being as much as I feel he should." Recognizing this aspect of Love is below her expectations, she rates this anecdote as Fair. For the third anecdote, Eileen states: "If I'm having a bad day at work, I don't get upset as much as I used to, because my love for him keeps me from getting too down." She rates this anecdote as Excellent.

Starting on Page 159 there are examples of anecdotes from the other five Love Categories that Eileen mapped, which will help you better understand how to map Love.

On Page 164 is a blank Section E form for you to use (Form 11). When mapping a Love Category for the first time, you can choose any of the six categories you'd like. After you have mapped one category, you can choose either to continue mapping other Love Categories or proceed directly to the next section. If you choose to map more categories now, go to www.matemap.com, click on "Exercise Forms," and print out as many copies of Form 11 as you need. Alternatively, you can photocopy Form 11 from Appendix B. If you choose to proceed to the next section, you can go back to map other Love Categories later. Remember, the more categories you map, the better you'll understand what you are looking for and the better prepared you'll be to make the best relationship decisions for yourself.

Go ahead now and return to the beginning of this section, referring to the instructions as you complete Section E.

Section E

Example 1

| Love Category 1 |
| What You Feel |
| Measure how he or she makes you feel. |

Provide three anecdotes and rate each one.

Anecdote 1		
Whenever I'm with him I feel safe and secure.	Excellent	✓
	Very Good	
	Good	
	Fair	
	Poor	
	None	

Anecdote 2		
He doesn't actively look out for my well-being as much as I feel he should.	Excellent	
	Very Good	
	Good	
	Fair	✓
	Poor	
	None	

Anecdote 3		
If I'm having a bad day at work, I don't get upset as much as I used to, because my love for him keeps me from getting too down.	Excellent	✓
	Very Good	
	Good	
	Fair	
	Poor	
	None	

Section E

Example 2

> Love Category I
> Importance
> Measure how important of a role he or she plays in your life.

Provide three anecdotes and rate each one.

Anecdote I		
	Excellent	
	Very Good	✓
	Good	
I factor in what he would want in most decisions I make, whether the decisions directly affect him or not.	Fair	
	Poor	
	None	

Anecdote 2		
	Excellent	
	Very Good	✓
	Good	
When talking to my girlfriends I refer to him (almost bragging about him) several times throughout our discussion.	Fair	
	Poor	
	None	

Anecdote 3		
	Excellent	✓
	Very Good	
	Good	
I am willing to compromise on issues that I wouldn't have compromised on previously, because I want him to get his way also.	Fair	
	Poor	
	None	

Section E

Example 3

> **Love Category 3**
> **What You Find Special (Or Not Special)**
> Measure what it is that makes you love him or her.

Provide three anecdotes and rate each one.

Anecdote 1		
He becomes interested in what interests me, even if it's not something he'd ordinarily care about.	Excellent	✓
	Very Good	
	Good	
	Fair	
	Poor	
	None	

Anecdote 2		
He's usually in touch with my emotions.	Excellent	
	Very Good	
	Good	✓
	Fair	
	Poor	
	None	

Anecdote 3		
He tells it like it is, whereas others distort the truth to avoid hurting my feelings, which doesn't really help me.	Excellent	
	Very Good	✓
	Good	
	Fair	
	Poor	
	None	

Section E

Example 4

> **Love Category 4**
> **Love Fulfillment**
> Measure how well this Love fits with what you expect Love to be.

Provide three anecdotes and rate each one.

Anecdote 1		
	Excellent	
	Very Good	
	Good	
I know I love him, but I'm unsure if he completely fills my love needs.	Fair	✓
	Poor	
	None	

Anecdote 2		
	Excellent	✓
	Very Good	
	Good	
I'm comfortable exposing my fears and vulnerabilities to him.	Fair	
	Poor	
	None	

Anecdote 3		
	Excellent	
	Very Good	
	Good	
I still feel the need to date multiple men.	Fair	
	Poor	✓
	None	

Section E

Example 5

<table>
<tr><td colspan="2" align="center">Love Category 5
Love Compatibility
Measure how well he or she fits with you.</td></tr>
</table>

Provide three anecdotes and rate each one.

Anecdote 1		
	Excellent	✓
	Very Good	
	Good	
Our relationship is the number one priority for both of us.	Fair	
	Poor	
	None	

Anecdote 2		
	Excellent	✓
	Very Good	
	Good	
He values the things about me that I value most about myself.	Fair	
	Poor	
	None	

Anecdote 3		
	Excellent	
	Very Good	
	Good	
I don't fully understand why he is in love with me.	Fair	✓
	Poor	
	None	

Section E
Example 6

Love Category 6
Changes My Outlook For The Better (Or Worse)
Measure how he or she changes your outlook.

Provide three anecdotes and rate each one.

Anecdote 1		
Knowing that someone so wonderful loves me makes me look at myself in a more positive way.	Excellent	✓
	Very Good	
	Good	
	Fair	
	Poor	
	None	

Anecdote 2		
Sometimes his pessimism rubs off on me.	Excellent	
	Very Good	
	Good	
	Fair	✓
	Poor	
	None	

Anecdote 3		
With his emotional support, I'm no longer afraid to try new things.	Excellent	✓
	Very Good	
	Good	
	Fair	
	Poor	
	None	

Section E

Love Category

Provide three anecdotes and rate each one.

Anecdote 1		Excellent	
		Very Good	
		Good	
		Fair	
		Poor	
		None	

Anecdote 2		Excellent	
		Very Good	
		Good	
		Fair	
		Poor	
		None	

Anecdote 3		Excellent	
		Very Good	
		Good	
		Fair	
		Poor	
		None	

CHAPTER

11

Phase III—
Calculating Your Status

In Phase II, your assessment of Personality Fit (Sections A and B), Magnetism (Sections C and D) and Love (Section E) was made using your judgment and opinions and then placing them into a rating system with six options: Excellent, Very Good, Good, Fair, Poor and None. Now, in Phase III (Section F), you will convert these descriptive ratings into percentages, which in turn will give you a snapshot of how compatible you are with your mate.

Section F should only be completed after you have mapped at least nine attributes (three Profile, three Spectrum and three Physical) and six category anecdotes (three Chemistry and three Love, if applicable). This will allow for your Mate

Map to have enough data on it to render it useful. Continue to read through Phase III now, even if you have not yet mapped the requisite amount of attributes and category anecdotes, so that you'll understand the process before you return to it later.

The Law of 80%

The Law of 80% states that, before starting a relationship, and anytime thereafter, we need to believe—*truly* believe— that each Relationship Essential meets a minimum of 80% of what we are looking for in a mate. If the 80% threshold is not met for all three Essentials separately, then this person is not right for us.

To illustrate the idea of the Law of 80%, picture three empty drinking glasses lined up side-by-side on your kitchen counter. The glass on the left represents Personality Fit, the glass in the middle represents Magnetism, and the glass on the right represents Love. The top rim of each glass represents 100% of what you are looking for in a relationship. The ideal scenario is to have all three glasses filled to the rim. In our quest to achieve 100%, the highest possible level, we also need to have a percentage that is considered to be the lowest acceptable threshold for choosing a mate. This threshold percentage is 80%. So in our drinking-glass scenario, each glass has to be filled to at least the 80% level before we decide that this person is the right mate for us. When the 80% level is met or exceeded, it can be said that we have *achieved* the Relationship Essentials.

The Law of 80% should be used as a guideline only. It should not be used as a strict rule, because, by nature, our judgments aren't exact. For example, knowing if something sits right with you to a 75% level versus a 85% level can be virtually impossible. The exact number is not important. What is important is that for each Essential, the overall threshold tends to be at around the 80% level or higher.

Once you have rated your level for each Essential, you can then make decisions based on this information. For example, if you have levels of 55%, 32%, and 47% for Personality Fit, Magnetism and Love, respectively, a relationship with this person is not a good idea. If you have levels of 88%, 83%, and 90% for Personality Fit, Magnetism and Love, respectively, this is an indication that this person may be right for you. To reiterate a point from an earlier section, keep in mind that the more thorough your Mate Map is, the more accurate an indicator it is. In addition, the length of a relationship is a factor in how thorough you can be. For example, if you have gone on four dates with someone, you obviously do not know him or her as well as if you have dated for four months.

Fluctuation Happens

During the course of a relationship, especially during the early going, the percentage levels often fluctuate, which is fine. What's important is that over time you achieve and sustain at least an 80% level for each Essential.

Iris, 38, has been dating Ben, 36, for three months. Iris rates Personality Fit at 90%. Just a month ago she would have rated it at 80%. This significant increase in such a short amount of time occurred as a result of a recent vacation the couple took together. They had five days of quality time and, the more Iris got to know Ben, the more she liked his personality and found it to be compatible with hers.

Iris rates Magnetism at 65%. When the relationship began, Iris rated her Physical Attraction to Ben at 85%, but over the past few months the attraction has declined. Perhaps she just doesn't find herself as attracted to him as she did when they first started dating. Or perhaps Ben has gotten too comfortable in their relationship and no longer cares about his appearance. Iris needs to figure out the reasons for the decline and whether she thinks the level of Physical Attraction can return to previous levels, or go even higher.

Iris is not in Love with Ben, so it is too early for her to assess Love, but Iris recognizes that, if she doesn't achieve Love with Ben at some point, she won't want to be in a relationship with him.

Be True to Your Assessment

Within the definition of the Law of 80%, you may or may not have noticed the inclusion of the word "truly." Here is the definition again: The Law of 80% states that before starting a relationship, and anytime thereafter, we need to *truly* believe that each of the Relationship Essentials meets a minimum of 80% of what we are looking for in a mate. The reason the word "truly" is significant is that sometimes our overall drive to be in a relationship clouds our view of the person we are involved with. For some irrelevant reason we may really want to end up in a relationship with this particular person, leading us to rate the person higher than we would otherwise. Or maybe we are so eager to be in a relationship that we look at any potential mate through rose-colored glasses.

Marcy, 25, and Mark, 27, have been in a relationship for one and a half years. The couple gets along incredibly well.

She rates their Personality Fit at 95%, their Magnetism at 95% and their Love at 80%. Marcy has had serious boyfriends in the past, but Mark is by far the one she likes the most. But, however much she likes Mark, Marcy is not in Love with him. Her Love rating of 80% is not genuine; she fudged it because she wants to be in Love with Mark so badly. She rationalizes her rating of 80% by thinking that she may fall in Love with him some day because the other components of their relationship work so well.

Although it is possible that, over time, Marcy will fall in Love with Mark, she needs to rethink the relationship. If she never falls in Love with him and they remain together, they are likely to eventually have problems, because Love, as one of the three Essentials, is a critical part of any relationship.

Relationship Status

Your relationship status is a snapshot of the current health of the relationship and is an indicator of whether or not your mate is the right person for you. At any point in a relationship, you are in one of three statuses: Green Light status, Yellow Light status or Red Light Status.

Green Light status: You have Green Light status if all three Essentials are 80% or higher. Your goal should be for your relationship to always be in Green Light status, which is an indicator that you are with a person who keeps you sufficiently happy and fulfilled. It is also a sign that you should consider moving forward with the relationship.

Yellow Light status: You have Yellow Light status if any one of the three Essentials is below 80%. Yellow Light status, means there are one or more major problems, or several minor problems in the relationship. If this is the case, you should try to improve the problem areas and bring the relationship to Green Light status. In Chapter 12, you will learn how to improve your problem areas. You should not remain in Yellow Light status indefinitely. After you complete the Mate Map, set a reasonable timeframe for getting to Green Light status. If you don't achieve Green Light status within your timeframe, then you should end the relationship.

Red Light status: You have Red Light status if two or three of the Essentials are below 80%. Red Light status means there are many problems in the relationship. If this is the case, you should try to improve the problem areas as soon as possible, to avoid wasting time and emotional energy. Your goal is to bring the relationship to Green Light status, or at least to Yellow Light status for the time being. If the problems cannot be resolved, you owe it to yourself to end the relationship so that you will be free to find someone with whom you are compatible.

In Step 3 of the instructions for Section F, you will learn how to use the Law of 80% to derive your relationship status.

Mapping Instructions for Section F

These instructions refer to the example, which starts on Page 175.

Description

In Section F, you will first assign percentages to Personality Fit, Physical Attraction, Chemistry and Love. Then you will assess your relationship using the Law of 80%, which will give you your relationship status.

Instructions

Read through these instructions once, then read them again as you complete Form 12, which starts on Page 178.

Take a brief look right now at the example for Section F that begins on Page 175 (Step 1) and continues on Pages 176 and 177 (Steps 2 and 3). This will give you a sense of how the calculations work before reading through the instructions. Although numbers are involved, you'll find the calculations are really only simple arithmetic. Just read through the instructions and follow along with the example. While the calculations are easy, using a calculator will make it easier still.

Step 1

There are four sections within Step 1: Personality Fit, Physical Attraction, Chemistry and Love. In the example, we'll review how to calculate Personality Fit; however, the instructions are the same for all four sections.

For the first section, Personality Fit, refer to your filled-out forms for the attributes you mapped in Section A3 (Form 7) and Section B3 (Form 8) as part of Chapter 10. You will be combining rating categories for both the Profile and the Spectrum Attributes.

The first column to the far left is labeled **Rating** and contains the six ratings that you are familiar with: Excellent, Very Good, Good, Fair, Poor, and None. The second column, **Rating Score**, lists the percentage associated with each rating—**Excellent = 100%, Very Good = 85%, Good = 70%, Fair = 50%, Poor = 30%**, and **None = 0%**. You'll notice each rating score is shown as a whole number instead of a percentage because this is the format needed for the calculations. The third column is called **Number of Attributes Mapped**, and is a tally of the attributes you mapped so far, grouped by rating. The fourth column is called **Aggregate Score**, and is an intermediate calculation on your way to assigning percentages.

Count up how many attributes you have for each rating (Excellent, Very Good, Good, and so forth). Write each of these totals in the appropriate space in the column marked Number of Attributes Mapped.

In the example (Page 175), Samantha, the 34-year-old real estate agent, is mapping her boyfriend Zach, 34. Including the Spectrum Attributes of Responsible–Irresponsible and Energetic–Mellow, she has also mapped twelve other Profile or Spectrum Attributes (not shown). She rated four as an Excellent fit, four that were Very Good, three she deemed Good, two she judged Fair, one she felt was Poor, and zero she judged None (No Fit).

When you have filled in the spaces under Number of Attributes You Mapped, multiply the number of attributes in each row by the Rating Score in each respective row. Write the resulting number in the fourth column, marked Aggregate Score. Note that whole numbers are used here too instead of percentages. Here, Samantha's numbers going down the column are: 400, 340, 210, 100, 30 and 0.

After you calculated the Aggregate Score for each of the six ratings, add up the numbers in that column, and then add up the numbers in the Number of Attributes You Mapped column. Here, the total Aggregate Score is 1,080 and the total Number of Attributes Mapped is 14. Next, Samantha takes the total Aggregate Score (1,080) and divides it by the total Number of Attributes Mapped (14) to get 77.14. If the resulting number ends with .5 or higher, round up by increasing the number by one and eliminating everything to the right of the decimal point.

Otherwise, round down by keeping the number the same and deleting everything to the right of the decimal point. Here, the number 77.14 is rounded down to 77. Finally, a percentage sign is added, giving Samantha a Personality Fit of 77%.

Repeat the above process for Physical Attraction (Section C), Chemistry (Section D) and Love (Section E). Note that for Chemistry and Love, the fourth column is called the Number of Category Anecdotes Mapped rather than the Number of Attributes Mapped.

When you have finished the calculations in Step 1 for the areas of Personality Fit, Physical Attraction, Chemistry and Love, move on to Step 2.

Step 2

Write the percentages you determined in Step 1 into the appropriate spaces.

In the example, Samantha writes in 77% for Personality Fit, 91% and 81%, respectively, for Physical Attraction and Chemistry and 82% for Love. Since Physical Attraction and Chemistry comprise Magnetism, their percentages need to be averaged. To determine the percentage for Magnetism, Samantha first adds the numbers (not the percentages) for Physical Attraction and Chemistry. This calculation yields 172, which she divides by two, giving her 86. She then adds a percentage sign, resulting in a Magnetism percentage of 86%.

Once you have a percentage for each of the three Relationship Essentials—Personality Fit, Magnetism and Love—it's time to apply these percentages to the Law of 80%. In the column marked **80% or Higher**, write in "Yes" for each Essential that is 80% or higher and "No" for each Essential that is below 80%.

Here Samantha writes in "No" for Personality Fit as it is 77% and thus lower than 80%, and "Yes" for both Magnetism and Love, as their percentages of 86% and 82%, respectively, are higher than 80%.

Step 3

Here you will determine if your relationship has Green Light, Yellow Light or Red Light status. If all three Essentials are rated 80% or Higher, you have Green Light status and can feel free to pursue this relationship. If one of the Essentials is rated less than 80%, the relationship is in Yellow Light status, and you should proceed with caution. If two or all three Essentials rate below 80%, you have Red Light status. If you have Red Light status and are unable to get to Yellow Light status, and eventually to Green Light status, after Phase IV of the Mate Map, you should move on to another relationship. Place a checkmark in the appropriate box to denote your relationship status.

In the example, Samantha sees that in Step 2, one Essential (Personality Fit) is ranked below 80%, and she places a checkmark in the Yellow Light status box.

Starting on Page 178 is a blank Section F form for you to use (Form 12). You can also print out a copy of Form 12 from www.matemap.com by clicking on "Exercise Forms" and following the simple instructions. Alternatively, you can photocopy Form 12 from Appendix B.

Go ahead now and return to the beginning of this section, referring to the instructions as you complete Section F.

Section F

Example

(1 of 3)

Step 1   Calculation of Percentages
Fill in the attributes you mapped and complete the calculations.

Personality Fit   (Sections A & B)

Rating	Rating Score		Number of Attributes Mapped		Aggregate Score
Excellent	100	X	4	=	400
Very Good	85	X	4	=	340
Good	70	X	3	=	210
Fair	50	X	2	=	100
Poor	30	X	1	=	30
None	0	X	0	=	0
TOTALS			14		1,080

Aggregate Score (divided by)	1,080 /
Number of Attributes Mapped	14
Personality Fit %	77%

Physical Attraction   (Section C)

Rating	Rating Score		Number of Attributes Mapped		Aggregate Score
Excellent	100	X	6	=	600
Very Good	85	X	3	=	255
Good	70	X	0	=	0
Fair	50	X	1	=	50
Poor	30	X	0	=	0
None	0	X	0	=	0
TOTALS			10		905

Aggregate Score (divided by)	905 /
Number of Attributes Mapped	10
Physical Attraction %	91%

Section F

Example

(2 of 3)

Step I Calculation of Percentages
Fill in the category anecdotes you mapped and complete the calculations.

Chemistry   (Section D)

Rating	Rating Score		Number of Category Anecdotes Mapped		Aggregate Score
Excellent	100	X	8	=	800
Very Good	85	X	5	=	425
Good	70	X	0	=	0
Fair	50	X	4	=	200
Poor	30	X	I	=	30
None	0	X	0	=	0
TOTALS			18		1,455

Aggregate Score (divided by)	1,455 /
Number of Category Anecdotes Mapped	18
Chemistry %	81%

Love   (Section E)

Rating	Rating Score		Number of Category Anecdotes Mapped		Aggregate Score
Excellent	100	X	9	=	900
Very Good	85	X	3	=	255
Good	70	X	2	=	140
Fair	50	X	3	=	150
Poor	30	X	I	=	30
None	0	X	0	=	0
TOTALS			18		1,475

Aggregate Score (divided by)	1,475 /
Number of Category Anecdotes Mapped	18
Love %	82 %

Step 2 Summary of Percentages
Copy in the percentages from Step 1 to the area below
and then record whether each is 80% or higher.

Relationship Essential	%	80% or Higher
Personality Fit	77 %	No
Physical Attraction	91 %	
Chemistry	+ 81 %	
Total	172	
Divided by 2	/ 2	
Magnetism	86 %	Yes
Love	82 %	Yes

Step 3 Relationship Status
Determine your relationship status based on Step 2.

Definitions

Green Light		All three Essentials are 80% or higher.
Yellow Light	✓	One Essential is less than 80%.
Red Light		Two or three Essentials are less than 80%.

Section F
Form 12

(1 of 3)

Step 1 Calculation of Percentages
Fill in the attributes you mapped and complete the calculations.

Personality Fit   (Sections A & B)

Rating	Rating Score		Number of Attributes Mapped		Aggregate Score
Excellent	100	X	____	=	____
Very Good	85	X	____	=	____
Good	70	X	____	=	____
Fair	50	X	____	=	____
Poor	30	X	____	=	____
None	0	X	____	=	____
TOTALS			____		____

Aggregate Score   (divided by) _____/____
Number of Attributes Mapped _____
Personality Fit % _____ %

Physical Attraction   (Section C)

Rating	Rating Score		Number of Attributes Mapped		Aggregate Score
Excellent	100	X	____	=	____
Very Good	85	X	____	=	____
Good	70	X	____	=	____
Fair	50	X	____	=	____
Poor	30	X	____	=	____
None	0	X	____	=	____
TOTALS			____		____

Aggregate Score   (divided by) _____/____
Number of Attributes Mapped _____
Physical Attraction Fit % _____ %

Section F

Form 12

(2 of 3)

Step 1 Calculation of Percentages
Fill in the category anecdotes you mapped and complete the calculations.

Chemistry   (Section D)

Rating	Rating Score		Number of Category Anecdotes Mapped		Aggregate Score
Excellent	100	X	_____	=	_____
Very Good	85	X	_____	=	_____
Good	70	X	_____	=	_____
Fair	50	X	_____	=	_____
Poor	30	X	_____	=	_____
None	0	X	_____	=	_____
TOTALS			_____		_____

Aggregate Score (divided by)   _____ /
Number of Category Anecdotes Mapped _____
Chemistry %   _____ %

Love   (Section E)

Rating	Rating Score		Number of Category Anecdotes Mapped		Aggregate Score
Excellent	100	X	_____	=	_____
Very Good	85	X	_____	=	_____
Good	70	X	_____	=	_____
Fair	50	X	_____	=	_____
Poor	30	X	_____	=	_____
None	0	X	_____	=	_____
TOTALS			_____		_____

Aggregate Score (divided by)   _____ /
Number of Category Anecdotes Mapped _____
Love %   _____ %

Step 2   Summary of Percentages
Copy in the percentages from Step 1 to the area below
and then record whether each is 80% or higher.

Relationship Essential	%	80% or Higher
Personality Fit	_____	_____
Physical Attraction	_____	
Chemistry	_____	
Total		
Divided by 2	/ 2	
Magnetism	_____	_____
Love	_____	_____

Step 3   Relationship Status
Determine your relationship status based on Step 2.

Definitions

Green Light		All three Essentials are 80% or higher.
Yellow Light		One Essential is less than 80%.
Red Light		Two or three Essentials are less than 80%.

12

Phase IV—Hot Spots and Action Plan

After determining your percentages and relationship status in Chapter 11 (Phase III), you are now ready to identify the hot spots in your relationship. A hot spot is defined as any problem in a relationship. So how do you identify hot spots? It's actually quite easy, because you've unknowingly already identified them! A hot spot is indicated by any attribute (Profile, Spectrum, Physical) or category anecdote (Chemistry, Love) you rated as Good, Fair, Poor or None. In terms of percentages, a hot spot is any area of your Mate Map where the percentage is below 80%. After identifying your hot spots, the next step is to create an action plan for eliminating or at least improving them.

If you have yet to complete Phase III, you'll be unable to do Phase IV, but read through it so that you understand the process for when you return to it later.

Mapping Instructions for Section G

These instructions refer to the example that begins on Page 186 (Steps 1–5) and continues on Page 187 (Steps 6–10).

Description

In Section G, you will note your hot spots, determine possible ways to improve them, take action on your hot spots if appropriate, and then track any change in rating.

Instructions

Read through these instructions once, then read them again as you complete Form 13, which starts on Page 196.

The first three steps help you identify a hot spot.

Step 1

Copy in any attribute or category anecdote from Sections A3, B3, C3, D or E that you found to be Good, Fair, Poor or None. Here we'll revisit the example used in Section A3 (Page 131), where Debbie, the 28-year-old graphic designer who is mapping Jason, 27, copies in the Profile Attribute **Age**.

Step 2

From Section A3, copy in the rating you originally chose for this attribute, also known as your **Original Fit** rating. Here Debbie places a checkmark in the box next to Fair.

Step 3

From Section A3, copy in the comments you originally wrote about this attribute. Here Debbie writes: "I'm uncomfortable with him being two younger than me, as my past boyfriends were all at least three years older than me."

The next two steps help you identify what possible action can be taken to improve the hot spot.

Step 4

Identify what you can do to fix the hot spot by describing any action you can take. Here Debbie writes: "Accept the age difference and don't have it bother me."

Step 5

Identify what your mate can do to fix the hot spot. Here, since her boyfriend is unable to change his age, she writes: "Nothing."

The next three steps help you to track what action was taken. Note that these steps do not take place right after you complete Steps 4 and 5, because you first need to allow time for reflection and action.

Step 6

Write in whether you took the action described in Step 4. Here Debbie writes: "I realized that I'm not completely comfortable yet with the age difference, but I may become so."

Step 7

Write in whether or not you discussed this hot spot with your mate, what was discussed, and the reason for your decision.

Here Debbie writes: "No, I did not discuss this with my mate because there is nothing he could do about it."

Step 8

Write in what your mate did as a result of Step 7. Here, since no discussion took place, Debbie writes, "N/A," which is short for Not Applicable.

The last two steps are for determining the New Fit for an attribute or category anecdote. The New Fit is simply an updated percentage along with updated comments.

Step 9

Now that you have taken action on your hot spot, rate the New Fit with your mate by choosing the appropriate box on the familiar six-point scale. It is possible for the New Fit to stay the same, improve or even get worse after you have completed Steps 1–8. Here, since Debbie has increased her comfort level with the age difference, she rates the New Fit as Good, an improvement from her original rating of Fair.

Step 10

Write in any comments you have regarding your New Fit. Here Debbie writes: "I'm more comfortable with the age difference, but I need to become even more comfortable with it."

There are four other examples of Section G starting on Page 188—one each for Spectrum Attributes, Physical Attributes, Chemistry and Love. Each example is a continuation of an example or category anecdote from Sections B3 (Page 136), C3 (Page 141), D (Page 147), and E (Page 161).

Starting on Page 196 is a blank Section G form for you to use (Form 13). When you have completed it, you can choose either to continue mapping other hot spots you have or proceed directly to the next section. If you choose to map more hot spots now, go to www.matemap.com, click on "Exercise Forms," and print out as many copies of Form 13 as you need. Alternatively, you can photocopy Form 13 from Appendix B. If you choose to proceed to the next section, you can go back to map other hot spots later. Keep in mind the more hot spots you map, the more likely you'll be to improve the compatibility with your mate.

Go ahead now and return to the beginning of this section, referring to the instructions as you complete Section G.

Section G

Profile Attribute Example

(1 of 2)

Identify The Hot Spots

Step 1   Hot Spots

Copy in any attribute from Section A3 that you found to be Good, Fair, Poor, or None.	Profile Attribute Age

Step 2   Original Fit Rating

Copy in the rating you originally chose for this attribute.	Good (70%) Fair (50%) ✓ Poor (30%) None (0%)	

Good	(70%)	
Fair	(50%)	✓
Poor	(30%)	
None	(0%)	

Step 3   Original Fit Comments

Copy in the comments you originally wrote about this attribute.	I'm uncomfortable with him being two years younger than me, as my past boyfriends were all at least three years older than me.

Possible Action

Step 4   What I Can Do

Describe any possibilities for action.	Accept the age difference and don't have it bother me.

Step 5   What My Mate Can Do

Describe any possibilities for action.	Nothing.

What Action Was Taken

Step 6   What I Did

| Provide description and rationale. | I realized that I'm not completely comfortable yet with the age difference, but I may become so. |

Step 7   Did I Discuss With My Mate

| Provide answer, what was discussed and why it was discussed. | No, I did not discuss this with my mate because there is nothing he could do about it. |

Step 8   What My Mate Did

| Provide description and rationale. | N/A |

Determine The New Fit

Step 9   New Fit Rating

Rate your New Fit with your mate by making a checkmark next to the appropriate rating to the right.	Excellent	(100%)	
	Very Good	(85%)	
	Good	(70%)	✓
	Fair	(50%)	
	Poor	(30%)	
	None	(0%)	

Step 10   New Fit Comments

| Write in any comments about your New Fit with your mate. | I'm more comfortable with the age difference, but I need to become even more comfortable with it. |

Section G

Identify The Hot Spots

Step 1   Hot Spots

Copy in any attribute from Section B3 that you found to be Good, Fair, Poor, or None.	Spectrum Attribute Responsible—Irresponsible

Step 2   Original Fit Rating

Copy in the rating you originally chose for this attribute.	Good	(70%)	
	Fair	(50%)	
	Poor	(30%)	✓
	None	(0%)	

Step 3   Original Fit Comments

Copy in the comments you originally wrote about this attribute.	Last week he showed up a half hour late for my important business dinner and was underdressed. This week he said he would take care of making plans for my birthday and never did.

Possible Action

Step 4   What I Can Do

Describe any possibilities for action.	Be more clear in communicating my expectations and what is important to me.

Step 5   What My Mate Can Do

Describe any possibilities for action.	Make a concerted effort to be more responsible.

188

Section G

Spectrum Attribute Example

(2 of 2)

What Action Was Taken

Step 6   What I Did

Provide description and rationale.	I've been more clear in my communications.

Step 7   Did I Discuss With My Mate

Provide answer, what was discussed and why it was discussed.	Yes, I mentioned several situations where he was irresponsible and suggested what I would like him to do to become more responsible.

Step 8   What My Mate Did

Provide description and rationale.	He recognized that he was wrong and agreed to improve.

Determine The New Fit

Step 9   New Fit Rating

Rate your New Fit with your mate by making a checkmark next to the appropriate rating to the right.

Excellent	(100%)	
Very Good	(85%)	
Good	(70%)	✓
Fair	(50%)	
Poor	(30%)	
None	(0%)	

Step 10   New Fit Comments

Write in any comments about your New Fit with your mate.	Two months after our conversation, he has become much more responsible, but he still needs further improvement.

Section G

Physical Attribute Example

(1 of 2)

Identify The Hot Spots

Step 1   Hot Spots

Copy in any attribute from Section C3 that you found to be Good, Fair, Poor, or None.	Physical Attribute Height

Step 2   Original Fit Rating

Copy in the rating you originally chose for this attribute.	Good	(70%)	
	Fair	(50%)	✓
	Poor	(30%)	
	None	(0%)	

Step 3   Original Fit Comments

Copy in the comments you originally wrote about this attribute.	She is taller than I would like. I'm 5'10" and when she wears heels she is taller than me, which makes me uncomfortable.

Possible Action

Step 4   What I Can Do

Describe any possibilities for action.	Get comfortable with the height difference.

Step 5   What My Mate Can Do

Describe any possibilities for action.	If she avoided wearing shoes with very high heels when we are together, it would make me feel more comfortable.

What Action Was Taken

Step 6   What I Did

Provide description and rationale.	I thought about why the height difference bothers me.

Step 7   Did I Discuss With My Mate

Provide answer, what was discussed and why it was discussed.	Yes, I asked her if she could try to wear lower heels when we are together. But I didn't let her know the extent to which this issue bothers me.

Step 8   What My Mate Did

Provide description and rationale.	She agreed to wear lower heels, but stated that, when she wears certain outfits, she will still wear shoes with at least a two-inch heel.

Determine The New Fit

Step 9   New Fit Rating

Rate your New Fit with your mate by making a checkmark next to the appropriate rating to the right.	Excellent (100%)	
	Very Good (85%)	
	Good (70%)	
	Fair (50%)	✓
	Poor (30%)	
	None (0%)	

Step 10   New Fit Comments

Write in any comments about your New Fit with your mate.	The practical side has improved slightly, but I still need to get to a comfortable place in my head.

Section G

Chemistry Example

(1 of 2)

Identify The Hot Spots

Step 1   Hot Spots

Copy in any category anecdote from Section D that you found to be Good, Fair, Poor, or None.	Chemistry Verbal Communication

Step 2   Original Fit Rating

Copy in the rating you originally chose for this category anecdote.	Good	(70%)	
	Fair	(50%)	✓
	Poor	(30%)	
	None	(0%)	

Step 3   Original Fit Comments

Copy in the comments you originally wrote about this category anecdote.	For some reason, when it comes to talking about our relationship, I don't open up as much as I should.

Possible Action

Step 4   What I Can Do

Describe any possibilities for action.	Understand why I'm not forthcoming so that I can take steps to communicate more openly.

Step 5   What My Mate Can Do

Describe any possibilities for action.	Nothing right now. But perhaps I'll ask him to adjust something if I think the problem is caused by him.

Section G

What Action Was Taken

Step 6   What I Did

Provide description and rationale.	I realized the primary reason why I'm not forthcoming is that when I opened myself up in my last relationship, several problems emerged that were detrimental to that relationship.

Step 7   Did I Discuss With My Mate

Provide answer, what was discussed and why it was discussed.	No, because I need to figure out some things. Eventually a discussion may need to take place.

Step 8   What My Mate Did

Provide description and rationale.	N/A

Determine The New Fit

Step 9   New Fit Rating

Rate your New Fit with your mate by making a checkmark next to the appropriate rating to the right.	Excellent	(100%)	
	Very Good	(85%)	
	Good	(70%)	
	Fair	(50%)	✓
	Poor	(30%)	
	None	(0%)	

Step 10   New Fit Comments

Write in any comments about your New Fit with your mate.	Now that I understand the problem better, I need to figure out how to overcome it.

193

Section G

(1 of 2)

Identify The Hot Spots

Step 1   Hot Spots

Copy in any category anecdote from Section E that you found to be Good, Fair, Poor, or None.	Love Love Fulfillment

Step 2   Original Fit Rating

Copy in the rating you originally chose for this category anecdote.	Good (70%)	
	Fair (50%)	✓
	Poor (30%)	
	None (0%)	

Step 3   Original Fit Comments

Copy in the comments you originally wrote about this category anecdote.	I know I love her, but I'm unsure if she completely fills my love needs.

Possible Action

Step 4   What I Can Do

Describe any possibilities for action.	Think through specifically what I feel is missing.

Step 5   What My Mate Can Do

Describe any possibilities for action.	Nothing.

Section G

Love Example

What Action Was Taken

Step 6   What I Did

| Provide description and rationale. | I started comparing the levels of Love between a past relationship and my current one. |

Step 7   Did I Discuss With My Mate

| Provide answer, what was discussed and why it was discussed. | No. |

Step 8   What My Mate Did

| Provide description and rationale. | N/A |

Determine The New Fit

Step 9   New Fit Rating

Rate your New Fit with your mate by making a checkmark next to the appropriate rating to the right.	Excellent	(100%)	
	Very Good	(85%)	
	Good	(70%)	
	Fair	(50%)	✓
	Poor	(30%)	
	None	(0%)	

Step 10   New Fit Comments

| Write in any comments about your New Fit with your mate. | No progress yet. |

Section G

Form 13

(1 of 2)

Identify The Hot Spots

Step 1   Hot Spots

Copy in any attribute or category anecdote from Sections A3, B3, C3, D or E that you found to be Good, Fair, Poor, or None.	

Step 2   Original Fit Rating

Copy in the rating you originally chose for this attribute or category anecdote.		

Good	(70%)	
Fair	(50%)	
Poor	(30%)	
None	(0%)	

Step 3   Original Fit Comments

Copy in the comments you originally wrote about this attribute or category anecdote.	

Possible Action

Step 4   What I Can Do

Describe any possibilities for action.	

Step 5   What My Mate Can Do

Describe any possibilities for action.	

What Action Was Taken

Step 6   What I Did

Provide description
and rationale.

Step 7   Did I Discuss With My Mate

Provide answer, what was
discussed and why it was
discussed.

Step 8   What My Mate Did

Provide description
and rationale.

Determine The New Fit

Step 9   New Fit Rating

Rate your New Fit with your
mate by making a checkmark
next to the appropriate rating
to the right.

Excellent	(100%)	
Very Good	(85%)	
Good	(70%)	
Fair	(50%)	
Poor	(30%)	
None	(0%)	

Step 10   New Fit Comments

Write in any comments
about your New Fit with
your mate.

13

Phase V—Reassessment

After you have worked to resolve any hot spots (Phase IV), the fifth and final phase of your Mate Map is Reassessment. The purpose of Reassessment is to review the areas you tried to improve and determine any progress that was made. If you have read through Phase IV but have yet to identify and take action on your hot spots, then you will not be able to complete Reassessment until you have done so. However, read through this chapter so you'll know what to do when you are ready.

Mapping Instructions for Reassessment

We're going to look at Reassessment by revisiting a previous example from Section F (Calculating Your Status), which was originally presented starting on Page 175 and appears with modifications starting on Page 202.

Description

In this section, Reassessment, you will track any rating for an attribute or category anecdote that changed as a result of completing Phase IV. You will also recalculate your percentages for the Relationship Essentials and determine if there is a change in your relationship status.

Instructions

Read through these instructions once, then read them again as you return to your completed Form 12 and do your Reassessment.

Step 1

Refer to Section G and identify any hot spots where the New Fit rating is different from the Original Fit rating. This can be done by comparing Step 2 (Original Fit rating) with Step 9 (New Fit rating) for any attribute or category anecdote you mapped in Section G. For any area of Section G that had at least one change in rating, update the number in the appropriate box in the Number of Attributes Mapped column by crossing out the old number and writing in the new number.

In the Reassessment example, which starts on Page 202, Samantha, the 34-year-old real estate agent who is mapping her boyfriend Zach, 34, found that the rating improved for two of her hot spots relating to Personality Fit. For the Spectrum Attribute **Responsible–Irresponsible**, the rating went from Poor to Good and for the Spectrum Attribute **Compromises–Doesn't Compromise** (not shown), the rating went from Fair to Good. In the column marked Number of Attributes Mapped, Samantha crosses out the original number of Good ratings, 3, and writes in the new number of Good ratings, 5. She also adjusts the numbers of the Fair and Poor ratings, which each decreased by one. For Fair, she crosses out 2 and replaces it with 1, and for Poor, she crosses out 1 and writes in 0. In the Aggregate Score column, Samantha recalculates the new totals for Good, Fair and Poor. She then crosses out the original Aggregate Score of each, and writes in the new Aggregate Scores, 350, 50 and 0, respectively. Next, Samantha crosses out the total Aggregate Score of 1,080 and replaces it with the new total of 1,140. She then divides 1,140 by 14, the Number of Attributes Mapped, to get 81.43, which becomes a Personality Fit percentage of 81%. Samantha then crosses out the original Personality Fit percentage of 77% and writes in the updated 81%.

Repeat the above process for Physical Attraction (Section C), Chemistry (Section D) and Love (Section E) for any hot spots whose New Fit rating is different than its original Fit rating. Note that for Chemistry and Love, the fourth column contains the Number of Category Anecdotes Mapped rather than the Number of Attributes Mapped. With Samantha, since she has not improved upon any hot spots pertaining to Chemistry or Love, these sections, which are on the second page of Section F, are not shown here.

Step 2

Write any changes to the percentages in Step 1 into the appropriate spaces in Step 2.

On Page 202, Samantha crosses out the original 77% for Personality Fit and writes in the new Personality Fit % of 81%.

For any Essential where the percentage changed, check to see if it increased to 80% or higher or decreased below 80%. If there is a change, cross out the original designation and write "Yes" or "No," respectively, in the appropriate blanks.

Here, since the Personality Fit percentage has exceeded the 80% threshold, Samantha crosses out "No" and writes "Yes" into the appropriate box in the 80% or Higher column.

Step 3

If there is a change in your relationship status, cross off the checkmark in the original status and place a checkmark in the box that represents your new status.

Glancing at the new Summary of Percentages in Step 2, Samantha can see that all three Relationships Essentials are now 80% or higher. So she crosses out the checkmark in the box marked Yellow Light status and happily checks off her new Green Light status.

Now that Samantha knows she is very compatible with Zach, she is more comfortable with moving their relationship forward. Furthermore, having gone through a comprehensive assessment of her needs and her relationship with Zach, Samantha now has greater peace of mind compared to the time before she used the Mate Map.

Still, Samantha must recognize that with percentages of 81% (Personality Fit), 86% (Magnetism) and 82% (Love), their relationship still has room for improvement.

Go ahead now and return to the beginning of this section, referring to the instructions as you complete your Reassessment.

Section F
Example
(1 of 3)

Step 1 Calculation of Percentages
Fill in the attributes you mapped and complete the calculations.

Personality Fit   (Sections A & B)

Rating	Rating Score		Number of Attributes Mapped			Aggregate Score	
Excellent	100	X	4		=	400	
Very Good	85	X	4		=	340	
Good	70	X	~~3~~ 5		=	~~210~~	350
Fair	50	X	~~2~~ 1		=	~~100~~	50
Poor	30	X	~~1~~ 0		=	~~30~~	0
None	0	X	0		=	0	
TOTALS			14			~~1,080~~	1,140

Aggregate Score   (divided by)   ~~1,080~~ / 1,140
Number of Attributes Mapped   14
Personality Fit %   ~~77%~~ 81%

Physical Attraction   (Section C)

Rating	Rating Score		Number of Attributes Mapped		Aggregate Score
Excellent	100	X	6	=	600
Very Good	85	X	3	=	255
Good	70	X	0	=	0
Fair	50	X	1	=	50
Poor	30	X	0	=	0
None	0	X	0	=	0
TOTALS			10		905

Aggregate Score (divided by)   905 /
Number of Attributes Mapped   10
Physical Attraction Fit %   91%

Step 2 Summary of Percentages
Copy in the percentages from Step I to the area below
and then record whether each is 80% or higher.

Relationship Essential	%		80% or Higher	
Personality Fit	~~77 %~~	81%	~~No~~	Yes
Physical Attraction	91 %			
Chemistry	+ 81 %			
Total	172			
Divided by 2	/ 2			
Magnetism	86 %		Yes	
Love	82 %		Yes	

Step 3 Relationship Status
Determine your relationship status based on Step 2.

Definitions

Green Light	✓	All three Essentials are 80% or higher.
Yellow Light	✓	One Essential is less than 80%.
Red Light		Two or three Essentials are less than 80%.

14

The Ongoing Mate Map

The purpose of creating your personal Mate Map is not only to provide you with immediate help in your current dating or relationship situation, but also to provide you with an ongoing reference tool. You are likely to find that your Ideal Inventory will be relevant for years to come because the desired attributes you seek in a mate will probably not change dramatically. However, it is likely that your desires will change somewhat and, fortunately, the Mate Map will evolve with you.

You can do periodic checks of your relationship using the Mate Map as often as you like, but it can be especially helpful during times when you are uncertain if your mate is right for you, or if there are emerging problems in your relationship. At the *very least*, I recommend that you review your Mate Map every six months. By doing so, you'll be able to identify any areas where improvements have been made, determine any areas that still need improvement and discover any new problem areas that have emerged.

Depending on the status of your relationship (Green Light, Yellow Light or Red Light) and the length of the relationship, the frequency with which you should review your Mate Map may vary. For example, if you've been in a relationship with someone for six months and you're in Green Light status, you may want to assess your compatibility every two months. If this relationship is in Yellow Light status, you may want to refer to your Mate Map every month. If this relationship is in Red Light status, you may want to refer to your Mate Map every two weeks. Keep in mind that the exact timing is not important. What's important is that over time you should continue to refer to your Mate Map, but the less compatible you are with your partner, the more often you should refer to it.

Here are a few different ways other people have approached going back to their Mate Map. Follow the approach you're comfortable with, or establish your own approach.

Update Approach 1: Start with blank forms and create a new Mate Map without first referring to your original Mate Map.

Update Approach 2: Review your original Mate Map first to get a sense of it and then refer to it while filling in blank forms.

Update Approach 3: Update your original Mate Map by writing your latest thoughts on it. It may be helpful to date these updates on your Mate Map by using a pen with a different color of ink. This way you'll know which comments are from your original Mate Map and which ones are from your latest version.

Whichever approach you use, the next step is to compare your new Mate Map with your original. By doing so, you will see how you and your relationship have evolved over time.

If you are in a relationship I recommend that, in addition to monitoring your Mate Map, you re-examine your relationship decision. By this I mean that just because at one point you decided that someone is the right person for you, it doesn't mean that this person will automatically continue to be right for you. People change and situations change, which can lead to an incompatible relationship. Sometimes there is simply nothing you can do about a relationship that ends up not working out. But, if you are not careful, you can make a bad situation worse. For example, you could be in a great relationship for a long time, but eventually you and your mate could drift apart. **As long as all indications are that this person is right for you, then you should work intensely to make the relationship work**. In other words, if the latest version of your Mate Map still has a level of at least 80% for Personality Fit, Magnetism and Love, then you should not give up on the relationship.

Introducing Your Mate to the Mate Map

If you are in a relationship that's in Green Light or Yellow Light status, you should consider introducing the Mate Map to your significant other so he or she can have the benefit of understanding the relationship better. If your relationship is in Red Light status, you may not want to inform your mate about the Mate Map, because any efforts your mate makes to improve the relationship may be futile.

Introducing the Mate Map to your mate may seem risky—what if your mate decides that you're not compatible with him or her? Although this concern is understandable, there's a more positive way to consider the situation. If using the Mate Map leads your mate to conclude that he or she no longer wants to be in a relationship with you, it is not because the Mate Map created the mismatch, but that incompatibility problems already existed. The Mate Map simply brought them to your attention. This is far better than the alternative, where you build a life with someone and years later your mate realizes he or she is unhappy and unfulfilled and ends the relationship at that time. Ignorance is not bliss. The sooner both you and your mate each examine what's important to you and how compatible you are, the better off your relationship will be.

The best way to introduce someone to the Mate Map is to use a direct approach. Tell your mate you heard about this system called the Mate Map, you used it and found it to be helpful, and you would like him or her to use it as well. Offer a specific example of how the Mate Map helped clarify an area of your relationship. For example, you might say, "The Mate Map helped me to appreciate how sincere and affectionate you are, as well as how compatible our chemistry is." By giving a specific example that shows the benefit of the Mate Map to the relationship, your mate is more likely to want to learn about the Mate Map.

Closing Thoughts

Please think of the Mate Map as I do, as a continuing tool that you may not refer to for weeks or months, yet can always use whenever the need arises. By thinking in terms of Personality Fit, Magnetism and Love, and by keeping your Ideal Inventory in mind, you have the ability to assess a potential mate or your current mate on an ongoing basis. With the new knowledge you have acquired through this book, you are now prepared to enter into a loving, fulfilling, and long-lasting relationship with a person who you can be certain is the right one for you.

The Mate Map Study

About the Mate Map Study

Below are excerpts from the Mate Map Study, which was conducted in early 2002 by Steven Sacks under the supervision of psychologist and statistician Dr. James A. Twaite.

Objectives of the Study

To show using quantitative and qualitative data that the Mate Map is effective at:

1. Increasing users' ability to know what is important to them in a mate.
2. Increasing their confidence in being able to choose a mate that is right for them.
3. Helping to identify and improve the problem areas in relationships.

Design of the Study

In January and February 2002, people who were either single or were in an unmarried relationship were invited to participate in a free 2½ hour Mate Map workshop in New York City. The workshop was advertised through magazines, flyers, email lists and websites. There were no other qualifications besides the relationship status criteria mentioned above. Participants registered for the workshop either through an online registration process or in person. Each participant was asked to complete a registration form, a pre-workshop questionnaire, and a post-workshop questionnaire. The registration data showed that the age range of the participants was 20–49. At the workshop, after participants learned about the Relationship Essentials, they completed the Mate Map exercises. The information that the participants provided within their personal Mate Maps was not collected for use in this study. Participants agreed that their names from the registration forms and questionnaires would be held strictly confidential, whereas their aggregate information could be used.

Pre-Workshop Data

Before examining how effective the Mate Map was in reaching the study's objectives, it is important to understand the attitudes and beliefs of the study participants. Here are some noteworthy responses from the pre-workshop questionnaires:

- 94% were concerned that they will never meet the right person.
- 93% were concerned that they don't know what's important to them in a mate as well as they should.

- 90% were concerned that their relationship won't last.
- 81% were concerned that they may not be with the right person.
- Of those respondents who reported that they had ended a relationship before, more than half (59%) said they had waited too long to end the relationship.

Post-Workshop Data

The post-workshop questionnaire contained thirteen questions concerned with the impact of the Mate Map experience on the respondents. Here are the participants' responses to the thirteen questions:

- 87% stated the Mate Map increased their confidence in understanding what the most important aspects of a relationship are to them.
- 75% stated the Mate Map increased their confidence in being able to choose the right mate.
- 77% stated the Mate Map increased their confidence in being able to improve a relationship by identifying and fixing problem areas (e.g., hot spots).
- 71% stated the Mate Map increased their confidence in knowing if they are with a person who is wrong for them.
- 70% stated the Mate Map increased their confidence in not staying in a bad relationship for too long.
- 91% agreed or strongly agreed with the majority of the ideas that are part of the Mate Map.
- 95% found the Mate Map exercises for the Profile Attributes to be helpful.
- 98% found the Mate Map exercises for the Spectrum Attributes to be helpful.

- 86% found the Mate Map exercises for Physical Attraction to be helpful.
- 91% found the Mate Map exercises for Chemistry to be helpful.
- 84% found the Mate Map exercises for Love to be helpful.
- 91% found the Mate Map exercises for the hot spots and action plan to be helpful.
- 84% indicated that they would recommend or strongly recommend the Mate Map to a friend.

Besides the quantitative answers, there was an open-ended question: "What's the most important thing you learned from the Mate Map?" Here is a sample of the comments provided in response to this question:

"I learned to be more specific and identify what is most important to me."

"That it's really important to think about all aspects of a relationship."

"The exercises enabled me to focus on my relationship and my needs."

"It is important to write down your thoughts. By answering some of the questions it helps you clear some things in your head."

"To focus on problems in relationships, not ignore them."

"To be clear about what is important to me at the beginning of a relationship and talk about issues early in the process."

"That you could evaluate relationships quantitatively."

"I must work at the relationship to make it last."

"How important the small nuances in a relationship are."

"Relationships are a process with many components—all equally important."

"To be more objective in assessing my relationships."

"Listing out the pros and cons and putting weights to them."

"It helped me address specific hot spots."

"To value Magnetism as an equally important part of relationships as Love and Personality."

"Chemistry and Physical Attraction are important; I didn't think they were in the past."

"To be very specific and realize certain attributes I thought were superficial really aren't."

"It is a scientific approach to finding a mate."

"Learning to assess what's really important to me in a person and what the 'dealbreakers' are."

On the questionnaire, participants were given the opportunity to provide testimonials in praise of the Mate Map. Here is a sample of the testimonials:

"Interesting analysis and way of filtering the black and white out of the gray area of relationships."

"I went from just jumping from relationship to relationship, not knowing why it doesn't work to now realizing I must take steps to make any relationship work."

"This workshop helped me focus on the things I want in a relationship instead of just settling for what I can get."

"Organized, practical and easy to use."

"An interesting concept for formalizing relationship assessment quantitatively."

"The Mate Map requires work, but so does any good relationship."

"I dragged my boyfriend to this: he thought it was great! He said there were many things he never thought about before and now understood what was important to him. In addition, it wasn't as 'girly' as he thought it would be."

"You've given me great insight."

"I have read a lot of relationship books, but haven't come across anything as tangible as this one."

Conclusion

Based on the data presented, the Mate Map has met its three objectives and has proven to be an effective system for choosing a compatible mate.

When examining the data by demographic groupings (relationship status, gender, age, ethnicity, education level) there were no statistically significant differences. Therefore it can be concluded that the Mate Map was found to be effective, regardless of relationship status, gender, age, ethnicity or education level.

About the Supervisor

The evaluation study of the Mate Map was supervised by Dr. James A. Twaite, who has worked as a consultant on empirical research studies since 1973. Dr. Twaite has a Ph.D. in econometrics from The Fletcher School of Law and Diplomacy (Tufts/Harvard) and an Ed.D. in counseling psychology from Teachers College (Columbia). He is a member of Phi Beta Kappa and Sigma Xi, the Scientific Research Society of North America. He is the author of three books: *Introductory Statistics* (1979, Scott-Foresman), *The Black Elderly* (with Marguerite Coke, 1995, Haworth Press), and *Children of Divorce* (1998, Jason Aronson). He has authored or co-authored numerous research articles appearing in such journals as *The Journal of Psychiatry and Law, The American Journal of Orthopsychiatry, Social Work, The Journal of Child Sexual Abuse,* and *The Journal of Trauma and Dissociation.*

B

Exercise Forms

Section A1

Form I

Make a checkmark in one of the four boxes across
to identify the relative importance of each attribute to you.

Attribute No.	Page No.	Profile Attributes	Extremely Important	Very Important	Moderately Important	Slightly Important
1	62	Age				
2	62	Career/Job				
3	62	Education Level				
4	63	Ethnicity				
5	64	Geographic Desirability				
6	65	Religion				
7	65	Socioeconomic Status				
8	66	Hobbies/Interests				
(Add one)						
(Add one)						

Section A2

Form 2

Step 1	Write in an attribute you determined to be of high importance in Section A1.	Profile Attribute 1

Step 2	How important is this attribute to you?

Extremely Important	
Very Important	
Moderately Important	
Slightly Important	

Step 3	Ideally, what are you looking for (and not looking for)?	

Step 4	What are the reasons for your preference?	

Step 5	How flexible are you about your ideal?

Not Flexible (Dealbreaker)	
Slightly Flexible	
Moderately Flexible	
Very Flexible	
Extremely Flexible	

Section B1

Form 3

(1 of 2)

Make a checkmark in one of the four boxes across
to identify the relative importance of each attribute to you.

Attribute No.	Page No.	Profile Attributes	Extremely Important	Very Important	Moderately Important	Slightly Important
9	80	Able to Relax—Uptight				
10	81	Adaptable—Unadaptable				
11	81	Affectionate—Not Affectionate				
12	82	Assertive—Unassertive				
13	82	Calm—Hotheaded				
14	83	Compromises—Doesn't Compromise				
15	84	Decisive—Indecisive				
16	85	Disciplined—Has No Self-Control				
17	85	Down-To-Earth—Pretentious				
18	86	Energetic—Mellow				
19	86	Follows Rules—Is Rebellious				
20	87	Forgiving—Holds Grudges				
21	88	Handles Adversity Well—Handles Adversity Poorly				
22	89	High Career Ambition—Low Career Ambition				
23	89	High Maintenance—Low Maintenance				
24	90	High Sex Drive—Low Sex Drive				
25	90	Independent—Dependent				
26	91	Insecure—Secure				
27	92	Intelligent—Not Intelligent				
28	92	Jealous—Not Jealous				
29	93	Kind-hearted—Uncaring				
30	94	Makes Me Laugh—Doesn't Make Me Laugh				
31	94	Mature—Immature				

Section B1

Form 3

(2 of 2)

Make a checkmark in one of the four boxes across
to identify the relative importance of each attribute to you.

Attribute No.	Page No.	Profile Attributes	Extremely Important	Very Important	Moderately Important	Slightly Important
32	95	Neat—Messy				
33	96	Optimistic—Pessimistic				
34	96	Polite—Rude				
35	97	Private—Revealing				
36	98	Proactive—Procrastinating				
37	98	Realistic—Unrealistic				
38	98	Responsible—Irresponsible				
39	99	Romantic—Unromantic				
40	100	Saver—Spender				
41	100	Self-Aware—Not Self-Aware				
42	101	Selfish—Unselfish				
43	101	Sensitive—Thick-Skinned				
44	102	Sincere—Insincere				
45	102	Smokes—Doesn't Smoke				
46	103	Sociable—Not Sociable				
47	104	Supportive—Unsupportive				
48	104	Talkative—Quiet				
49	105	Trustworthy—Not Trustworthy				
50	106	Worldly—Naïve				
(Add one)						
(Add one)						
(Add one)						
(Add one)						

Section B2

Form 4

Step 1

Write in an attribute you determined to be of high importance in Section B1.

Spectrum Attribute 1

Left Pole Attribute

Right Pole Attribute

_____   _____

Step 2

How important is this attribute to you?

Extremely Important	
Very Important	
Moderately Important	
Slightly Important	

Step 3

Ideally, what are you looking for (and not looking for)?

Most	Very	Somewhat	Somewhat	Very	Most

Step 4

What are the reasons for your preference?

Step 5

How flexible are you about your ideal?

Not Flexible (Dealbreaker)	
Slightly Flexible	
Moderately Flexible	
Very Flexible	
Extremely Flexible	

Section C1

Form 5

Make a checkmark in one of the four boxes across
to identify the relative importance of each attribute to you.

Attribute No.	Physical Attributes	Extremely Important	Very Important	Moderately Important	Slightly Important	Examples
51	Hair					short, blonde, straight, balding
52	Eyes					brown, blue, big, oval-shaped
53	Face					round, square jaw, high cheekbones
54	Smile					eyes light up, shows teeth
55	Lips					full, thin
56	Teeth					straight, pearly white, has full set
57	Nose					big, small, narrow, flaring nostrils
58	Ears					big, small, stick out
59	Skin					olive, smooth, pasty white
60	Height					5'1", 5'8", 6'4"
61	Body					average frame, heavy, muscular
62	Sex Appeal					very sexy, not so sexy
63	Cuteness					very cute, not so cute
64	Pretty/Handsome					not pretty, quite handsome
65	Feminine/Masculine					very feminine, exudes masculinity
66	Overall Look					dresses well, natural, has tattoos
(Add one)						
(Add one)						

Section C2
Form 6

Step 1	
Write in an attribute you determined to be of high importance in Section C1.	Physical Attribute 1
	_____

Step 2 — How important is this attribute to you?

Extremely Important	
Very Important	
Moderately Important	
Slightly Important	

Step 3 — Ideally, what are you looking for (and not looking for)?

Step 4 — What are the reasons for your preference?

Step 5 — How flexible are you about your ideal?

Not Flexible (Dealbreaker)	
Slightly Flexible	
Moderately Flexible	
Very Flexible	
Extremely Flexible	

Section A3

Form 7

Step 1

Copy in the Profile
Attribute you chose
in Section A2.

Profile Attribute 1

_____

Step 2

Describe your mate.

Step 3

Describe your
Personality Fit.

Step 4

Rate your Personality Fit
with your mate by making
a checkmark next to
the appropriate category
to the right.

Excellent	
Very Good	
Good	
Fair	
Poor	
None	

Section B3

Form 8

Step 1

Copy in the Spectrum Attribute you chose in Section B2.

Spectrum Attribute 1

Left Pole Attribute | Right Pole Attribute

Step 2

Describe your mate.

Most	Very	Somewhat	Somewhat	Very	Most

Step 3

Describe your Personality Fit.

Step 4

Rate your Personality Fit with your mate by making a checkmark next to the appropriate category to the right.

Excellent	
Very Good	
Good	
Fair	
Poor	
None	

224

Section C3

Form 9

Step 1	Copy in the Physical Attribute you chose in Section C2.	Physical Attribute 1

Step 2	Describe your mate.	

Step 3	Describe your Physical Attraction Fit.	

Step 4	Rate your Physical Attraction Fit with your mate by making a checkmark next to the appropriate category to the right.	Excellent	
		Very Good	
		Good	
		Fair	
		Poor	
		None	

225

Section D

Form 10

Chemistry Category

Provide three anecdotes and rate each one.

Anecdote 1			
	Excellent	
	Very Good	
	Good	
	Fair	
	Poor	
	None	

Anecdote 2			
	Excellent	
	Very Good	
	Good	
	Fair	
	Poor	
	None	

Anecdote 3			
	Excellent	
	Very Good	
	Good	
	Fair	
	Poor	
	None	

Section E

Form 11

Love Category

Provide three anecdotes and rate each one.

Anecdote 1		
	Excellent	
	Very Good	
	Good	
	Fair	
	Poor	
	None	

Anecdote 2		
	Excellent	
	Very Good	
	Good	
	Fair	
	Poor	
	None	

Anecdote 3		
	Excellent	
	Very Good	
	Good	
	Fair	
	Poor	
	None	

Section F

Form 12

(1 of 3)

Step 1 Calculation of Percentages
Fill in the attributes you mapped and complete the calculations.

Personality Fit   (Sections A & B)

Rating	Rating Score		Number of Attributes Mapped		Aggregate Score
Excellent	100	X	___	=	___
Very Good	85	X	___	=	___
Good	70	X	___	=	___
Fair	50	X	___	=	___
Poor	30	X	___	=	___
None	0	X	___	=	___
TOTALS			___		___

Aggregate Score (divided by) _____/_____
Number of Attributes Mapped _____
Personality Fit % _____ %

Physical Attraction   (Section C)

Rating	Rating Score		Number of Attributes Mapped		Aggregate Score
Excellent	100	X	___	=	___
Very Good	85	X	___	=	___
Good	70	X	___	=	___
Fair	50	X	___	=	___
Poor	30	X	___	=	___
None	0	X	___	=	___
TOTALS			___		___

Aggregate Score (divided by) _____/_____
Number of Attributes Mapped _____
Physical Attraction Fit % _____ %

Section F

Form 12

(2 of 3)

Step 1 Calculation of Percentages
Fill in the category anecdotes you mapped and complete the calculations.

Chemistry   (Section D)

Rating	Rating Score		Number of Category Anecdotes Mapped		Aggregate Score
Excellent	100	X	_____	=	_____
Very Good	85	X	_____	=	_____
Good	70	X	_____	=	_____
Fair	50	X	_____	=	_____
Poor	30	X	_____	=	_____
None	0	X	_____	=	_____
TOTALS			_____		_____

Aggregate Score   (divided by)   _____ / _____
Number of Category Anecdotes Mapped   _____
Chemistry %   _____ %

Love   (Section E)

Rating	Rating Score		Number of Category Anecdotes Mapped		Aggregate Score
Excellent	100	X	_____	=	_____
Very Good	85	X	_____	=	_____
Good	70	X	_____	=	_____
Fair	50	X	_____	=	_____
Poor	30	X	_____	=	_____
None	0	X	_____	=	_____
TOTALS			_____		_____

Aggregate Score   (divided by)   _____ / _____
Number of Category Anecdotes Mapped   _____
Love %   _____ %

Section F

Step 2 Summary of Percentages
Copy in the percentages from Step 1 to the area below
and then record whether each is 80% or higher.

Relationship Essential	%	80% or Higher
Personality Fit	_____	_____
Physical Attraction	_____	
Chemistry	_____	
Total		
Divided by 2	/ 2	
Magnetism	_____	_____
Love	_____	_____

Step 3 Relationship Status
Determine your relationship status based on Step 2.

Definitions

Green Light		All three Essentials are 80% or higher.
Yellow Light		One Essential is less than 80%.
Red Light		Two or three Essentials are less than 80%.

Section G

Form 13

(1 of 2)

Identify The Hot Spots

Step 1   Hot Spots

Copy in any attribute or category anecdote from Sections A3, B3, C3, D or E that you found to be Good, Fair, Poor, or None.	

Step 2   Original Fit Rating

Copy in the rating you originally chose for this attribute or category anecdote.	Good	(70%)	
	Fair	(50%)	
	Poor	(30%)	
	None	(0%)	

Step 3   Original Fit Comments

Copy in the comments you originally wrote about this attribute or category anecdote.	

Possible Action

Step 4   What I Can Do

Describe any possibilities for action.	

Step 5   What My Mate Can Do

Describe any possibilities for action.	

Section G

Form 13

(2 of 2)

What Action Was Taken

Step 6   What I Did

Provide description and rationale.	

Step 7   Did I Discuss With My Mate

Provide answer, what was discussed and why it was discussed.	

Step 8   What My Mate Did

Provide description and rationale.	

Determine The New Fit

Step 9   New Fit Rating

Rate your New Fit with your mate by making a checkmark next to the appropriate rating to the right.	Excellent	(100%)	
	Very Good	(85%)	
	Good	(70%)	
	Fair	(50%)	
	Poor	(30%)	
	None	(0%)	

Step 10   New Fit Comments

Write in any comments about your New Fit with your mate.	

C

Dating and Relationship Resources

Here is a list of websites of organizations that readers may find useful. Inclusion on this list does not mean that I endorse a particular company or its products or services. Readers must make their own independent evaluation of these resources and reach their own conclusions about them.

Online Dating Services

Istclassdating.com	Kiss.com	Metrodate.com
Absoluteagency.com	Lavalife.com	Mingles.com
Americansingles.com	Lovecity.com	Personals.Yahoo.com
Atlastwemeet.com	Makethematch.com	Singles.com
Casualkiss.com	Match.com	Singlesnet.com
Date.com	Matchamerica.com	Singleswithscruples.com
Dating.com	Matchcontact.com	Udate.com
Domeconnection.com	Matchdoctor.com	Unitedsingles.net
Dreamdates.com	Matchsinglescafe.com	Wejustclicked.com
Friendfinder.com		

Online Dating Services—Special Interests

Advancedegreessingles.com	*Advanced degrees*
Afroconnections.com	*African-American*

Blacksingles.com	*African-American*
Asiafriendfinder.com	*Asian*
Asiancircles.com	*Asian*
Sportmatesearch.com	*Athletic singles*
Catholicsingles.com	*Catholic*
Christiancafe.com	*Christian*
Christianmates.com	*Christian*
Christianpersonals.org	*Christian*
Meetchristians.com	*Christian*
Singlec.com	*Christian*
Singlechristian.com	*Christian*
Date-a-doc.com	*Doctors*
Natural-friends.com	*Environmental-minded*
Gay11.com	*Gay & Lesbian*
Gaysinglesonline.com	*Gay & Lesbian*
Theartfulmatchmaker.com	*Gay & Lesbian*
Latinmatcher.com	*Hispanic/Latino*
Latinoloveconnection.com	*Hispanic/Latino*
Jcupid.com	*Jewish*
Jdate.com	*Jewish*
Jewishmatch.com	*Jewish*
Jsingles.com	*Jewish*
Astralhearts.com	*Metaphysical/Spiritual*
Matrimonials.com	*Muslim & Indian*
Muslimmarriagejunction.com	*Muslim*
Lovemelovemypets.com	*Pet owners*
Single-parent-connection.com	*Single parents*
Single-parents-dating.com	*Single parents*
Singleparentspersonals.com	*Single parents*
Veggidate.com	*Vegetarians*

In-Person Dating Services

3minutedating.com	Itsjustlunch.com
8minutedating.com	Meetinggame.com
Great-expectations.com	Speeddating.com
Hurrydate.com	Take8.com

General Dating and Relationship Information

About.com/people	LifetimeTV.com
AOL.com (keyword: relationships)	Love.MSN.com
herPlanet.com	Oxygen.com
iVillage.com	Women.com

Glossary

Chemistry

The natural connection between two people, which includes such intangibles as nonverbal communication and sexual chemistry. Part of Magnetism.

Green Light status

Your relationship status if all three Essentials are 80% or higher. If you have Green Light status, you should feel free to pursue a relationship with this person.

Hot Spots

The problems in a relationship as indicated by any attribute or category anecdote you rated as Good, Fair, Poor or None. In terms of percentages, a hot spot is any area of your Mate Map where the percentage is below 80%.

Ideal Inventory

The shopping list of what you want in a mate. With this list, you have a valuable pool of information to use for shaping your relationship future.

The Law of 80%

This law states that, before starting a relationship, and any-time thereafter, we need to truly believe that each Relation-

ship Essential meets a minimum of 80% of what we are looking for in a mate. If the 80% threshold is not met for all
three Essentials individually, then this person is not right for
us.

Love

Having deep feelings of affection and emotional intensity
toward a potential or current mate, which include the elements of intimacy and exclusivity. One of the three Relationship Essentials.

Magnetism

The combination of Physical Attraction and Chemistry that
connects two people. One of the three Relationship Essentials.

The Mate Map

The system that helps us focus on the important details of
what we truly want in a mate and enables us to determine
how compatible we are with a particular person.

Mate Map Principles

The general guidelines that keep us focused on the overall
aspects of relationships that matter most, and are applied to
the Mate Map. The three Mate Map Principles are: fulfill
your needs, keep your balance between intuition and
rational thinking, and examine Personality Fit, Magnetism
and Love separately.

Nebulous Zone

The unstructured area where our dating and relationship
experience and beliefs are stored.

Personality Fit

The degree of fit between the personality attributes one person desires and the other person possesses. These personality attributes are divided into two groups: the Profile Attributes and the Spectrum Attributes. One of the three Relationship Essentials.

Physical Attraction

The strong, often passionate attraction that occurs when one person's Physical Attributes match what another person finds desirable. Part of Magnetism.

Physical Attributes

The aspects of one's physical appearance that you find appealing. Part of Physical Attraction.

Profile Attributes

Factual information about a person. Part of Personality Fit.

Red Light status

Your relationship status if two or three of the three Essentials are below 80%. If you have Red Light status, and you are unable to eventually reach Green Light status, you should seriously consider moving on to another relationship.

Relationship Essentials

The areas of a relationship where it is critical you achieve a high level of compatibility. The three areas are Personality Fit, Magnetism and Love.

Spectrum Attributes

Personality traits that comprise everything about our personalities from core values and beliefs to specific behaviors. Part of Personality Fit.

Yellow Light status

Your relationship status if any one of the three Essentials is below 80%. If you have Yellow Light status, you should proceed with caution.

Index

Acknowledgments

Much like the path to having a great relationship, the path to creating *The Mate Map* was accomplished by having the right people around me.

To Kathryn Lance, who helped transform my words into well-written prose, and made me a better writer in the process. Thank you for giving so much to this project.

To Dr. Bonnie Eaker Weil, who recognized how much the Mate Map system can help people in the many facets of mate selection. Thank you for being a champion for *The Mate Map*.

To Dr. James A. Twaite, who supervised the Mate Map Study. Thank you for collaborating with me to determine just how well the Mate Map works.

To Robyn Spizman, who provided me with valuable advice in putting together the book. Thank you for your guidance.

To Jamie Forbes, who helped fine-tune the text and instructions. Thank you for your thoroughness and detailed eye.

To Pamela Terry at Opus 1 Design, who helped me to create a fantastic cover and book jacket. Thank you for being so responsive.

To Barry Kerrigan and Del LeMond at Desktop Miracles, who did a wonderful job of designing the interior text and charts. Thank you for your attentiveness.

To Susan Kendrick, who helped develop the copy for the book jacket. Thank you for your wordsmithing talents.

To Paula Winicur, who provided beneficial advice for the cover. Thank you for your creativity and contribution.

To Peter Hurley, who directed me through my photo shoot. Thank you for making my picture look so good.

To John Kremer, who provided his book knowledge and experience. Thank you for sharing your expertise.

To Sallie Randolph, who provided me with legal advice. Thank you for your counsel.

To my parents, Elaine and Allan Sacks, who came out of retirement to help me with this project. You have always looked out for me and your love and support are unwavering. Thank you for the huge contribution you make in my life.

To my sister, Shari Sadler, who simultaneously nurtured me and tormented me during our childhood. Thank you for always looking out for me.

To my brother-in-law, Barry Sadler, who's been like the brother I never had. Thank you for taking such good care of my sister.

To my nephews, Justin and Jonathan Sadler. Thank you for helping me realize that you can do anything in life that you feel like doing.

To my aunt, Anita Sacks. Thank you for all of the wisdom and encouragement you provide.

To all of my friends. Thank you for your friendship over the years. And thank you for your patience and understanding over the past year. It's not that I replaced you with any new friends, it's just that I was busy creating the Mate Map.

To all of the people not mentioned here who helped me make this book a reality, I thank you.

To my girlfriend, Nikki. Thank you for all of your love and support during this project, both of which have been essential in bringing *The Mate Map* to life. I love you. I enjoy every day with you more and more—further confirming that I chose the right mate.

To everyone mentioned here, thank you for all of your hard work and for helping me put this book on the map.

About the Author

Steven Sacks is the creator of the Mate Map™ system and a noted expert on mate selection. Mr. Sacks is also a dynamic and highly sought-after speaker and consultant. He earned a B.S. in business from the State University of New York at Buffalo and an MBA from Fordham University. He splits his time between his hometown of New York City and Durham, North Carolina, with his girlfriend—the first Mate Map success story.

More About the Mate Map

Need help with your Mate Map? Want to take your Mate Map to the next level? You can consult with Mr. Sacks either in person or by phone. For information, send an email to consulting@matemap.com

Want to get a discount on bulk quantities of *The Mate Map* for your corporation, association, university, or other organization? Contact the sales department of Mate Map Enterprises at 212–592–9057 or send an email to info@matemap.com for details and discount information.